"An unusual and affecting memoir . . . sad and funny."—*New York Times*

"Funny and touching."—*Washington Post*

"What are the odds of such uncles?
And what are the odds of such a nephew
to do them justice? A rare book and a fine,
funny, moving, strange and sane one."
—Roy Blount, Jr.

•

"Heartbreaking and hilarious."—*Seattle Times*

"A Marx Brothers invasion of *Leave It To Beaver* . . .
a wonderful tale."—*Des Moines Register*

"A funny and charming memoir."—*Newsday*

"What a story! What a family!"—*Detroit Free Press*

"A crisply told, rollicking narrative."
—*Philadelphia Inquirer*

Unstrung Heroes

My Improbable Life
with Four
Impossible Uncles

Franz Lidz

A SIGNET BOOK

SIGNET
Published by the Penguin Group
Penguin Books USA Inc., 375 Hudson Street,
New York, New York 10014, U.S.A.
Penguin Books Ltd, 27 Wrights Lane,
London W8 5TZ, England
Penguin Books Australia Ltd, Ringwood,
Victoria, Australia
Penguin Books Canada Ltd, 10 Alcorn Avenue,
Toronto, Ontario, Canada M4V 3B2
Penguin Books (N.Z.) Ltd, 182–190 Wairau Road,
Auckland 10, New Zealand

Penguin Books Ltd, Registered Offices:
Harmondsworth, Middlesex, England

Published by Signet, an imprint of Dutton Signet, a division of Penguin Books USA
Inc. Previously published in a hardcover edition by Random House, Inc.

First Signet Printing, September, 1995
10 9 8 7 6 5 4 3 2 1

*Grateful acknowledgment is made to the following for permission to reprint previously
published material:*
JERRY VOGEL MUSIC CO., INC.: Excerpts from "Foolish Facts" by Frank Crumit. Copyright
1931 by Jerry Vogel Music Co., Inc. Reprinted by permission of Jerry Vogel Music Co.,
Inc., c/o Plymouth Music Company, Inc.
WARNER/CHAPPELL MUSIC, INC.: Excerpts from "Boobs in the Woods" (Carl Stalling).
Copyright 1948 Vitaphone Corp. (renewed). Copyright © 1976 Warner Bros., Inc.:
Excerpts from "Bath Tub Song" (Herb Magidson, Michael Cleary, Ned Washington).
Copyright © 1959 Vitaphone Corp. (renewed). Copyright © 1987 Warner Bros., Inc.
All rights reserved. Reprinted by permission.

Ⓟ   REGISTERED TRADEMARK—MARCA REGISTRADA

Printed in the United States of America

For Maggie and Carl

"The dilemma was thus of extreme simplicity: to go on, or to turn, and return, round the corner, the way he had come."
—Watt *(Samuel Beckett)*

ACKNOWLEDGMENTS

EXTRA special thanks to Carl Schoettler

Special thanks to Rob Buchanan, Kris Dahl, Susan Kamil, and John Turturro

Thanks to Schuyler Bishop, Annette Donato, Polly Freeman, Paul Gilbert, Christopher Guest, Joan Hammer, Nora Irvine, Manny Kramer, Bobbye Kolsky, Dick Lewis, Theodore Lidz, Celia LoPinto, Abraham Menashe, Mark Moskowitz, Catherine O'Hara, Mary Margaret O'Hara, John Papanek, Tracy Pappas, Rita Pinardo, Gerald Renner, Karen Rinaldi, Paul Somerson, Edmund Welles, and the Rockland Psychiatric Center

Chapter 1

Flipped Lidz

There once were five crazy brothers who grew up on the Lower East Side. Four turned into my uncles. One became my father.

Only Uncle Arthur and Uncle Harry are still alive, and they're old now. They live together in a sort of muttering disharmony. They ignore most of the rest of the world. But they get along famously with Gogo, my oldest daughter. At Gogo's third birthday party, Uncle Arthur gave her a box full of worn shoelaces. Uncle Harry sucked on a Camel and blew smoke into her face.

"Are you a dragon, Uncle Harry?" she asked. Gogo had never seen anyone smoke before.

She asked him for a drag.

"It'll make your teeth yellow," cautioned Maggie, her mother.

"I want to see Uncle Harry's yellow teeth."

"He don't have teeth," said Uncle Arthur through a mouthful of chocolate cake, "and you couldn't make him wear them if he did." Uncle Arthur was dressed in layers of Salvation Army overcoats kept closed with rusty safety pins. His pants were hemmed with duct tape. He had gentle brown eyes and twin dikes of silver hair holding the baldness at bay.

Uncle Harry looked like a down-and-out Cartier-Bresson. His scarf and beret were ratty, his double-breasted jacket shabby, his mustache wispy and weedy. He rolled the burning end of the Camel between his thumb and forefinger, then pinned onto Gogo's blouse a shiny button bearing a photo of himself. He'd inducted her into the Harry Lidz World Fan Club, of which he was not just the object of adulation, but founder, president and only other member.

"In Spain, Franco's men surrounded me," he said. "There were fifteen of them, big guys with big guns—cannons—and me, with just my fists. They aimed at me and fired—pop, pop, pop—not twenty feet away. There was no time to duck. I was wounded in the heart." He lifted his shirt to show her the spot. "My arms were broken. I couldn't raise them to touch my shoulders. My feet were broken, too."

"Wow, Uncle Harry!" said Gogo. "Did you die?"

"Die! Me?" said Uncle Harry with a mocking laugh. "Why, I knocked the tar out of them with my *chin*! Knocked the tar out of every one."

He was so taken with the idea of saving the Spanish Republic that he didn't notice he had planted his elbow in the chocolate.

"Uncle Harry!" Gogo said. "Your elbow's in your cake."

"Who cares?" he said, and plunked his other elbow in.

"Right, who cares?" said Gogo, and planted *her* elbows in *her* cake.

So for the rest of the afternoon these two comrades wore flecks of frosting on their elbows, like mud from the Spanish trenches.

When Uncle Harry and Uncle Arthur shuffled off to the train home, Gogo shouted, "Be good boys, OK?"

She looked sad, yet somehow gleeful. "I miss Uncle Arthur and Uncle Harry," she said.

"Do you want to go with them?"

"No, I don't want to go *with* them. I want to *miss* them."

Which I suppose is the way I've always felt about my uncles—their charm increased with their distance.

It was Gogo who made me think I should write about my uncles before they outlive what they mean to me, and time erases memory. Uncle Arthur and Uncle Harry have already outlived my mother and father and several generations of relatives and friends.

My uncles were smelly, screwy, astonishingly scrawny old guys who had abandoned everyday life. The world had packed them away in a back closet, like old sweaters. They still managed to pop up at the most inappropriate moments, subverting my

mother's insistence on good manners and personal
hygiene, and making a joke out of my father's cold,
scientific detachment. As a boy, I happily enlisted
in their conspiracy against sanity. Now, as I write
about these flickering men, I realize they kept me
reasonably sane.

Uncles—especially bachelor uncles—fill some
odd cranny in families. They provide a hideout from
the crushing commonplaces of our mothers and fathers. What do they know about kids? They give
odd presents, never useful, mostly eccentric. They
don't have to say no. It once seemed to me that every family I knew had at least three crazy uncles.
Now if you have one, you have to cherish him.

I had four: Uncle Leo the literary genius, Uncle
Danny the paranoid, Uncle Harry the self-
proclaimed world champ and Uncle Arthur the
connoisseur who had amassed the world's most ex-
haustive shoelace collection. They were at once
close and inaccessible. I never thought of them as
young, but they didn't seem as grown up as other
adults. They lived outside the mainstream—old
Reds who had survived the coffee house and delica-
tessen revolutions of the Lower East Side. My uncles were sons of immigrants, heirs of the *shtetl,* the
ghetto, the pogroms, dwellers outside the Pale. But
they were happy to be outsiders; they never had to
make the same compromises true adults did; they
remained innocent and faithful to their own loopy
dreams.

I needed my uncles' innocence and fantasy life

because reality became very harsh sometime after my seventh birthday. My mother began to die of cancer. They told her she had a year to live. But she lived until I was thirteen. My Aunt Joanie, her youngest sister, told me she held on for my Bar Mitzvah.

My memories of my mother are filtered through her suffering. She was in and out of hospitals. She had chemotherapy, radiation, a hysterectomy, an adrenalectomy, a double mastectomy. At home I heard her call out when she couldn't contain her pain. For years.

My father, the scientist, read everything about cancer, pushing the doctors to the edge of the experimentation. He tried to stave off death with science, just as he countered his brothers' madness with order and logic. He failed, inevitably, but he was tender and optimistic and he dressed her wounds with his own hands.

For six years our house was occupied by death. My parents never told me, but I knew. My little sister Sandy and I would peek through a crack in the bathroom door to watch my mother cauterize her running sores. We were fascinated and fearful, sorrowful and occasionally resentful. Even today I can barely sort out the conflicting emotions.

My mother was courageous, though sometimes I glimpsed something weary and resigned in her eyes. A strong woman who was accustomed to taking control of her life, she was unprepared for the way her cancer shattered it.

I, too, was unprepared, and in searching for ways
to escape the fact of my mother's illness, I relied in-
creasingly on the company of my uncles. They had
a reservoir of bewildered lunacy that was foreign to
my parents.

I could hardly wait for a festival or a birthday or
a Jewish holiday when Uncle Danny and Uncle Arthur would turn up like a pair of cracked mounte-
banks. Uncle Danny, who believed the world was
created to spite him, opened his arms and enfolded
me. I loved him the most because he told me some
of his secrets. In those days, Uncle Arthur was Uncle Danny's slow, silent sidekick. I liked his hugs a
lot less. He always had a faintly musty odor, and
sharp, sparse whiskers bristled from his chin. Uncle
Leo remained locked away in an asylum until he
died, and Uncle Harry didn't come out of his until
I was in high school.

When Danny and Arthur came to our house, we
mainly watched television together. My father, who
designed TVs for a living, wasn't much fun to look
at shows with. He watched like a technician, more
engrossed in the drizzling static than the program.
Uncle Danny used to talk back to the set, joining in
the action, quibbling with the answers on quiz
shows. Uncle Arthur was so quiet I could never tell
if he was awake.

My uncles and I would sit in the den where my
father had built the TV into a paneled wall. Three
on a couch, me in the middle, watching cartoons.
Uncle Danny liked Daffy Duck the best; how the

demented bird survived Bugs Bunny's tricks with an ingenuous cunning appealed to us both. We sang along:

> Oh, people call me Daffy,
> They think that I am goony,
> But just because I'm happy
> Is no sign I'm Looney Tuney.

Uncle Danny croaked out the verse in a fruity, giggly voice that I still conjure up with pleasure. I loved to sit with my uncles, warm between their frail, frail bodies; Uncle Arthur silent, Uncle Danny and I bouncing and rollicking away, our high-pitched voices curiously similar.

My father had no room in his life for his brothers' looney tunes. He skimmed along the edge of their self-absorption, seeing the same stars, but reading their message as a Man of Reason. He respected the laws of physics, mathematics . . . society. The youngest of the five Lidz brothers, he didn't for a minute plan to follow the other four over the brink. He had a job, a family, responsibilities.

Looking back, of course, I see my father's preoccupation with car compasses and electric toothbrushes as no less talismanic than Uncle Arthur's collection of coffee cans and dresser handles, or Uncle Harry's crazed correspondence. My father was a man of infinite gadgetry, and my legacy is a drawerful of hi-fi parts, reel-to-reel tapes and Super

8 movies. I listen to the tapes and watch the films, some poignant, some painful.

In the first film my father took of me, I'm sitting in a high chair, clutching a bottle. His floodlights are so intense that I lean to get out of their heat, and the high chair topples over. My father holds the camera on me and lets it run as I lie on the floor crying underneath the high chair. I wait for my mother to rush into the frame.

He documented the costume he made me wear for the second-grade Halloween parade: outfitted with crepe-paper wings and a huge papier-mâché head, I bumble along as a one-eyed, one-horned Flying Purple People-Eater, crashing into other kids in the procession; bobbing the monstrous head constantly to get my bearings. My father had spent an entire weekend creating the People-Eater, but forgot to leave holes for the eyes.

Cut to me running away from home, age seven. I remember putting on Uncle Danny's gray fedora and striding into the living room to announce my departure.

"I'm running away," I told my father. It was April, 1959. This was the first time my mother had gone to stay in the hospital. With my father in charge, Long Island had suddenly become oppressive.

I was pretty sure my father loved me, but I was never completely sure he loved me any more than he did a problem in theoretical physics. He was an electronics engineer, an inventor meticulous in his work, and he seemed to want everything, including

me, to be as precise and orderly as a table of loga-
rithms. I felt like a number, and not a prime
one—an insignificant one. Maybe twenty-eight.

"I mean it," I said. "I'm running away."

"Wait . . ." said my father.

I brightened.

". . . I'll get the movie camera."

Then came that little rush of salt in the nose that
makes you choke when you start to cry.

My father let the camera roll with the dispas-
sionate eye of an anthropologist filming an Amazo-
nian tribe. So I scuffle away from the camera,
looking back and looking back, a small figure beneath Uncle Danny's fedora. Slung over my shoulder is a hobo bag tied to a stick with the shoelaces
Uncle Arthur had gleaned—is gleaning still—from
the streets of New York. I watch the kid recede into
the distance and know now I'm watching through
my father's eyes. I feel this mournfulness for us
both.

I don't recall where I was going. I like to think it
was to see Uncle Danny and Uncle Arthur. But
how could a seven-year-old know whether the
Bronx was left or right? So I curled up on the back
seat of our Nash Rambler. I wondered if my father
had forgotten me. Would he call my mother? Would
she call the Missing Persons Bureau? She always
said she would if I ran away. I pulled Uncle
Danny's hat down over my eyes. I tried to sleep. I
got cold. I crept back to my bedroom.

My father's last surviving picture show is a snippet from my Bar Mitzvah. My mother looks sallow and stricken, her body defeated by cancer, bandages barely concealed by her chiffon blouse. She'll be dead in three months. She's forty-two. She wears a brave smile.

The oldest footage I have was taken by a long-forgotten photographer at my parents' wedding reception in 1950. It's a lilting swirl of toasts and laughs, dancing and embraces. Everybody's jammed into a long, narrow, smoky room, and the hard-edged camera lights swing from table to table, fixing the partygoers in a paralyzing glare. The film frames mysterious space—protean and labyrinthine, dark and glowing, glittering and dim. The smell of the bulb heating the celluloid, the popping of the sprockets, the dots, lines and crazy patterns wriggling across the screen, the snatches of brightly lit gaiety—these suffuse me with sadness.

Everybody is so young and I remember them all as being so old. The white-gloved flower girl flexing her fingers as if still anticipating the flung bouquet, that's Cousin Judy. But who are these wasp-waisted women cocking their cigarettes at Bette Davis angles and mincing about the room in their fur stoles—real, fake, indeterminate. And these gravy-eyed men shaking hands, patting each other on the back, getting drinks, offering food. Are they related to me?

Out of the smoke and silence I can almost hear the laughter and drifting conversation. I recognize my mother's mother, Nanny Ruth, a flighty, spoiled woman who left her three daughters penniless after draining off their trust funds. Nanny Ruth appears in a sinfully scarlet gown and matching, go-to-hell lipstick. Her third husband, Abe the used-car dealer, reaches across a couple of hundred pounds of belly and lubricates the occasion with a shot of Canadian Club. Two years later he will abscond with what little money my grandmother has left.

Here comes my father, bouncing across the screen, convivial and confident as a social director at a Catskills resort. He's courtly with the ladies, princely among the gentlemen, democratic with the catering crew. In this mood, he could probably make small talk with the couple on the cake. Suddenly, he breaks into the *kuzatski,* the wild Russian dance he did at every wedding. I hear the music in the whirring of the projector. The herky-jerky film speeds him up to dervish pace. A stray lock of hair drops across his forehead like a sprig of ivy over a tombstone. His gestures are disconcertingly familiar. I recognize the ones he passed on to me. I still mirror his sly half-smirk forty years later.

The willowy brunette my father flings around the dance floor is Selma Harris, my mother. She doesn't seem to be wearing any makeup, perhaps a dash of color over her eyes, which in the stark light are an extraordinary green-blue, an Adriatic blue. The long cut of her jaw is crisp and firm, and good lines fan from the edges of her eyes. Her complicated satin suit was made by my grandmother. She wears its fashionable peplum like an accolade.

The camera catches her twisting a napkin slowly over and over between her fingers. But I don't think she's nervous. She seems perfectly composed, at ease, not easily rattled. She looks heartbreakingly happy.

I'm adrift in a fog of melancholy when a figure catapults into the frame as if he were beamed down from the moon. Uncle Arthur. He wears a screechy bow tie, a white carnation and the look of a man in the fifty-fifth minute of Happy Hour. Oblivious to the camera, he bends down halfway across the dance floor to fuss with his shoelaces. His jacket is ill-fitting, and I can guess why. Its pockets are stuffed with toaster springs, bathtub stoppers, lengthy notes to himself in a squinty, hieroglyphic hand—oddments he finds indispensable for any occasion.

Uncle Danny's at the wedding, too, though at first I don't realize it because he's been hiding. The camera catches him in pieces: his ear, his hat, his baggy trousers, his shadow. Finally, it nails him full frame as he herds along his mother, the matriarch of this family of five sons. Uncle Danny looks like one of those nervous gunsels Elisha Cook, Jr., used to play in the forties movies, who drank too much coffee between midnight and three A.M. He raises his hand to shield his mother's eyes from the lights. She's a smiling, uncomfortable woman of enormous age. Her hands are embossed with veins, but her hair is thick and blue-black.

I freeze the frame to get a good look at Uncle

Danny. My cryptovoyeurism would confirm his extravagant and self-fulfilling paranoid fantasies: that a person who doesn't yet exist will someday analyze his every twitch and gesture. But the only way to study Uncle Danny is to isolate him, like a specimen on a slide. He looks glum and subdued and slightly embarrassed, as if his hosts have committed an unseemly indiscretion he'd rather not acknowledge. He doesn't approve of women other than his mother. And he may also be put off by Uncle Arthur, who totters around in a drunken frazzle—bleary, bemused, his eyes scrunched up in delight. In the movie's highlight, Uncle Arthur grabs my mother's best friend, spins her around in an impromptu jitterbug step and rips her dress, exposing her brassiere for film history.

The camera pans back to my parents, smiling and formal, a little vulnerable in the newness of their marriage. They're being sent off to their Miami honeymoon in a rain of rice. Uncle Danny, squeezed between Uncle Arthur and his mother, is trapped in the picture. The camera pushes in. Their faces fill the frame, as out of focus as memory. The frame goes white and the film sputters off the reel.

I shut off the projector. I put the reels back in their cases. I turn to the letters my father wrote me. I read them all. I hear his voice. I talk to Uncle Arthur and Uncle Harry and those who are left of their twenty-six first cousins. I sometimes feel like this story has been written from graveside conversations filled with fantastical anecdotes, well-worn gossip, profound illuminations—fragments that may or may not produce a rounded image, a whole person, the history of a family.

Chapter 2

Does the Name
Pavlov Ring a Bell?

My father would have made a splendid uncle. He was a happily mismatched kind of guy who'd wear a powder-blue sports coat, tan slacks, black wing-tips and a dark red plaid shirt with a pocketful of pens and Phillips screwdrivers. He assumed a faintly befogged professional mien, but he sparked with edgy energy as he talked. Everyone in our cozy Long Island hamlet—we lived in a neighborhood of Valley Stream called Green Acres—indulged him as Crazy Sid, the mildly crackpot inventor. He puzzled people with long-winded esoterica, exasperated them with excruciating wordplay, daunted them with oblique discourse. His talk caromed around more angles than the cue ball in three-cushion billiards. Our neighbors decided he was a genius so that they wouldn't have to listen too hard to what he was saying.

Of course, what is endearing in an uncle can be deplorable in a father. I don't think mine ever really worked out a philosophy for raising children. He believed mainly in the power and the purity of science, and assumed that, like everything else, human behavior could be conditioned and quantified. B. F. Skinner fascinated him long before anyone else knew modification from meditation.

Fortunately, my mother interceded before my father packed me away in a Skinner box. But one night when I was four he rigged up a contraption to cure me of bed-wetting. The wet sheets triggered an alarm that emitted a piercing shriek I knew alerted all of Green Acres. I woke up sweating, quaking, eyes filled with tears. Everyone—my mother, my father, my little sister—burst into my room to witness my shame. Years later I told my father of the absolute terror and self-loathing I had felt. He laughed. "You never wet your bed, again, did you?"

The bed-wetting gizmo was only one entry in the catalogue of my father's inventions. He designed electric toothbrushes, portable televisions, fiberglass violins, early Frisbees and ... much, much more, none of which brought him any lasting financial security. He always worked for some corporation that took the patents.

It bothered my mother more than my father that he never made any money from his inventions. She felt he was being cheated. But he was a purist concerned, as he once told me, with discovering the *It*. The four-pronged fork approached It. So did barbed wire. "It's as if it were destined before time," he said, "born through the hospital of each inventor." Yet he had refused to join the Manhattan Project, which involved the creation of the ultimate It, the atomic bomb. He told me, "I just couldn't do it."

The progeny he took most pride in was neither me nor Sandy, but a transistorized portable tape recorder he designed in 1956, when I was four. He later brought home his prototypes, no doubt to divert our attention from our mother's illness. He found communicating with us easier through an electronic intermediary. He sometimes bugged our conversations for posterity, like Nixon in the White House.

On one of the old reels from my youth, I quiz him about arithmetic. His answers come from the outer limits of mathematics.

"Dad," I say finally. "What's the highest number?"

"Since time and space are unbounded," he begins, "everything starts with nothing." An operation for polyps in his throat had left his voice gravelly and confidential, as if he had spent his childhood watching gangster movies, as if a bullet were caught in his craw. "Naturally, nothing begins and nothing ends, and nothing can be created out of nothing, and, as Socrates said, 'As for me, all I know is that I know nothing. . . .'"

"Dad," I cut in. "What's the highest number?"

"I'm getting to that," he continues, "but first I'll need to teach you some basic algebra. Let's define the limit that a function f approaches at $x = a$ when for x close to a, $f[x]$ is close to any preassigned . . ."

"Daddy!"

A long pause.

"Infinity," he says.

It was a weapon, this word, and I decided to brandish it one day at school. I'd always been a pretty quiet student, given over to dreamy introspection. All I ever wanted to be was a tap dancer, but somewhere along the line I got waylaid into kindergarten.

School for me was a combination of tedium and barbarism. I hated it. I still shudder when I recall the sound of tiny chairs scraping against Paleozoic linoleum; the incessant winking of fluorescent lights; the battle for dominance in the playground. I never understood my teachers' compulsion to stuff me with facts and figures, and then test me to see how many I'd retained. I'd read a question and get hung up on a word like *apricot,* and repeat it again and again in my mind until I hardly ever finished a test. Grades, scores, results: He who gave the most correct answers in the allotted time got the highest number, was judged the smartest. The first thing I did after I learned to multiply was figure how many days, hours, minutes, seconds of this I had to endure until graduation.

I was never particularly popular or unpopular until the day I stopped saying the Pledge of Allegiance. This was the idea of my father, the lapsed Socialist. Miss Glassman, my second-grade teacher, scowled at me but didn't say a word. Suddenly I felt a tide of mumbling resentment from my classmates. It was then, under siege, that I announced I knew the highest number.

"Oh yeah?" shouted Dicky Haas from the back of the class. "What?"

"Infinity."

Silence. Back then, that kind of inside information carried great weight. I exulted in my newfound celebrity.

During recess the following afternoon, Dicky challenged me: "My father says there's a number higher than infinity."

"Is not!"

"Is too!"

"Name it."

"Infinity squared."

I felt like I'd been slugged in the stomach.

"You butt!" I shot out.

He spat at me. I got him in a scissors hold and we began to scuffle. Miss Glassman broke it up. We demanded arbitration. Miss Glassman called in a sixth-grade math teacher, who ruled for infinity squared.

"Liar!" I screamed. Miss Glassman sent me home. I cried all the way. My father had betrayed me. I shut myself in my room and wouldn't come out, even for dinner.

Finally, my father came in. My head was buried under my pillow. He'd brought me thin, brown cigarettes—Thomas Jefferson Chums—and set them on the night stand next to my bed.

"You take puffs," he whispered. "Don't inhale."

I pretended I was asleep.

"There *is* one number that's higher than any

other," he said. I drew back the pillow to peek at him.

"It's higher than infinity squared or cubed, or even drawn and quartered."

"What is it?"

"Infinity to the infinity power."

When I got to school the next day, I unloaded my bombshell.

I was elected class president.

But there really wasn't much point in staying in school. As I explained to my father after the second week of third grade: "I think I know all I need to know. Can I quit and go to work with you?"

My father shook his head. "School will societize you," he said without much conviction.

I nodded, unconvinced.

My father remained Captain Marvel to me for a long time after that. He could peel an orange in one long spiral, tie a boatswain's knot and douse a candle flame with his fingertips. He had installed the first TV antenna atop the Empire State Building and climbed to its tip. He had dined on woolly mammoth steak with the directors of the American Museum of Natural History. He could repair a broken TV with a matchbook cover as easily as he could adjust a misplaced modifier in one of my English compositions. He even knew what a runcible spoon was and whether or not people could live on the sun.

Sports didn't quite fit into his quadratic equations. Only the Newtonian neatness of pool intrigued him. Yet he was a competent wrestler. You learn every hold when you're the youngest of five brothers. "I could pin them all," my father bragged. He taught me to wrestle and he pinned me, too. He'd lock me in a half nelson and we'd crash around my bedroom as I tried to get out. Sometimes I did—maybe he let me, but I loved it all the same.

He kept strong and trim by following a rigorous daily routine of sit-ups, jumping jacks and Marine Corps pushups. All this started on his fortieth birthday, when I was four. "I finished in twelve minutes," he exulted.

"Is that good or bad?" I asked.

"Good!"

A month later he said, "I'm down to eleven minutes."

"Wow!"

Over and over he'd tell me how he became the chin-up champion of his grade school on the Lower East Side. He was a squirty kid who couldn't even do one at the start of school in September, when he decided to become the champ. On the next day, he did one. On the third, two. By the end of the month, he was Chin-up King.

The first time I heard this tale I did one chin-up. The next day I didn't bother. Thirty chin-ups meant something to a little Jewish kid on the Lower East Side. Two chin-ups were a little boring in Green Acres, where I was as American as any other kid.

The most obsessive thing about my father was

his wordplay. During meals he'd pepper me with rotten food puns: "Lettuce now eat. Nobody beets me. That's mighty pea-culiar . . ." Every conceivable variation was squeezed out of whatever we were eating. ". . . You'll never ketchup. Don't be shell-fish . . ." My father could uncork weird comic demons, but there was a strain about his humor, like a funnyman who's afraid that his audience will go back to its cocktails and ignore him. He never knew when to quit. When nobody laughed, he rattled on and on, his puns more and more unlikely and unfunny.

If I wanted to talk to him, it had to be on his terms. I couldn't speak engineering, so I spoke punic. We'd engage in punny duels that were all parries and ripostes.

"Are termites boring?" he'd ask me.

"They mite be."

"To bee or not to bee . . ." Onward he buzzed: My father really didn't need me for an audience. I laughed—I always laughed—though I'd heard most of his repertoire about a hundred and nine times. As a child, I wondered why my mother never seemed to get the same barrage. She could penetrate the defenses of wordplay and scientific language to some inner place he had protected from everybody else.

When she invited my third-grade teacher over for dinner, she made my father promise to curb his tongue. "No religion. No politics. And watch the puns." She hid the heretical bookends my father, the devout atheist, kept on the mantel. He'd made them by sawing through a wooden knockoff of Durer's praying hands.

I liked Miss Clarke. She talked about the old kings back home in Britain, and I always admired men in capes. But I was uncomfortable eating dinner with her. There was something creepy about having your teacher over to your house, like some violation of the separation of powers.

"It'll be good for you," said my mother. "She'll get to know us."

"I don't want her to get to know us," I protested. "I don't want to have to *eat* with her. She's gonna watch us eat, Mom."

I could only be embarrassed. What if Miss Clarke told my mother I threw spitballs? What if my friends heard Miss Clarke had come to my house and had eaten dinner with me? What if my father told Miss Clarke I had wet my bed when I was four?

"Oh, don't be silly," my mother said. Schmoozing the teacher was part of her middle-class ethos.

She fixed a big feast, corn on the cob, asparagus and my favorite, chicken pot pie.

"Remember, watch the puns," she warned my father when Miss Clarke rang the doorbell. It was no use. My father's mind was a motor that didn't have an off switch.

"What part of England are you from?" asked my mother as we sat down to eat.

"I was raised in Nottingham," Miss Clarke replied.

"I was raised in Manhattan," said my father. "Fortunately, the rope broke."

"Robin Hood lived in Nottingham," I said.

"Very good," said Miss Clarke.

"Tell me," said my father. "When Robin Hood went to bed, did Friar Tuck him in?"

Miss Clarke smiled politely.

"Get me turtle soup, Selma," said my father, "and make it snappy."

My mother smiled politely.

Miss Clarke said she'd be taking my class on frequent visits to the public library. "I want my students to get in the habit of looking things up."

"That sounds terrific," said my mother.

"When I was a boy," said my father, "I'd go to the library to look up dresses."

My mother's brows fused in a deep furrow of displeasure. My father, however, had already launched a long arpeggio of corniness: "Ralph Will, Grant Wood, Frederick Schall, Bobby Shantz, Elaine May, Galerie Maeght, Kubla Khan." After a coy pause, he added, "But Immanuel Kant."

Miss Clarke seemed dazzled by this show of erudition. "You'd be a worthy candidate for Mensa, Mr. Lidz," she said.

"What's that?" asked my father. "A place for women who have problems with their periods?"

My mother raked a finger across her throat. My father smiled disingenuously. Miss Clarke blushed.

"Mensa is an intellectual social club in England," she said. "Membership is limited to people who have IQs in the top two percent of the world. And you have to take a test to prove it."

My father pursed his lips like a man about to spit out a prune pit. "If you want my opinion," he harrumphed, "anyone willing to take that test shouldn't be allowed to."

"The intelligent need each other, Mr. Lidz. If you are bright, no matter how many friends and relations you have, you need the challenge of intelligent and stimulating company to protect you from getting stale or too conceited. Mensa members talk about everything, but on a much higher plane. At my last meeting, we discussed the difference between Schwarzschild and Reissner-Nordstrom black holes."

"Black holes?" said my father. It was actually a subject he knew something about, but for once sarcasm triumphed over pedantry. "Almost lost the Rambler in a big one on Old Mill Road the other night. The DPW digging up the street again."

Miss Clarke tried again. "You would enjoy it. We use a lot of puns, a lot of plays on words. The conversation flits and flies. I never have to say anything twice unless my listener is deaf."

"Whaddja say?"

Miss Clarke mustered a small laugh, but her tolerance of my father's jokes was clearly dying. I felt like he was digging my grave.

"My father was a sailor," I broke in. "Like Popeye."

He began telling a story from his misspent youth: "One time my brother Arthur and me were hanging around the docks when a sailor asked us if we wanted chocolate. "Sure," we told him, and each swallowed a chunk. It turned out to be chewing tobacco. For the next three days we puked our guts out."

Miss Clarke considered the pot pie at the end of her fork, and genteelly lowered it to her plate.

"I smoke tobacco," I said. "Dad buys it for me."

"You purchase *cigarettes* for your son?" asked Miss Clarke, utterly aghast.

My father coughed, my mother choked.

"Don't worry," I said. "I just puff. I never eat them, do I Daddy?"

I did pass to fourth grade unscathed, but every time I raised my hand in Miss Clarke's class, she stared at it closely as if inspecting for nicotine stains.

My father made pacts with me. We'd be outlaws together and live outside the rules that women made. We pledged never to tell anyone our secrets, especially my mother. We tiptoed to the attic to share a shot of aquavit, or crept down to the basement, where he kept his rifle hidden. I would draw a bulls-eye on a page of looseleaf paper that he taped to the concrete wall. We leaned through the basement stairs like snipers in a gun slot and each fired off a round. Then we'd wait for my mother's scream: "What if it had ricocheted, Sid?" My father and I grinned at each other, buddies, reckless men.

My mother wasn't a spoilsport; she just didn't care to have me shot before my Bar Mitzvah. She wanted me to get good grades, she wanted me to be neat and clean, she wanted me to be nice to my teachers. I was, but I still wanted my father to sneak me cigarettes.

The day I announced to him I wanted to become a Webelo, his response was unequivocal.

"No! It's a dangerous precedent."

"It's harmless, Sid," my mother said. "Every boy in his class is a Webelo."

"It's the first stage of military brainwashing." My father always thought of the long-term effects.

"It's the Cub Scouts!"

"He'll learn to be a fascist."

"He'll learn to knot a necktie."

"Next he'll be enlisting in the Navy."

"*You* enlisted in the Navy!"

Her logic was impeccable. She became my den mother and I learned how to knot neckties and make ashtrays out of clam shells. When it came time to pick a new pack leader, I volunteered my father. "No, no, no," he protested. "Absolutely not." I pressured him, my mother pressured him, and eventually he gave in.

"But I won't wear a uniform," he insisted. And he didn't, though no one noticed.

My father invariably stood on principle and then stepped off in whatever direction my mother

pointed him. She had even engineered their court-
ship.

She talks about it on the only tape recording I
have that preserves her voice. "I was crazy about
him," my mother says. She speaks with low, firm
certainty. I listen and think I hear a woman who
knows her mind. "We might have started dating a
lot sooner if he wasn't—if he *weren't*—so myopic."

She picked up her nice feeling for the mysterious
subjunctive mood at Manhattan's Erasmus High
School. She was a Latin major who got a perfect
score on her Regents. She never went to college.
She accepted the responsibility of being the oldest
daughter of a slightly batty mother and went to
work at Nanny Ruth's dress shop on the Upper
West Side.

My mother wasn't pretty, but she had the sweet
good looks of the girls the boys left behind when
they shipped off for World War II. Her figure was
slim and rangy like Lauren Bacall's, and she had
the same skeptical grin. But she was a little gawky
and somewhat shy and retiring. Her sisters, Bobbye
and Joanie, remember she was dating less and less
as the fatal age of thirty approached.

She had to be brought out by her younger sister,
Joanie, the peppy one. Aunt Joanie taught her to
smoke and drink, and made her get her nose fixed.
When the dress shop went bust, my mother went
to work with Joanie at a Manhattan electronics firm
where my father was an engineer.

"He was a good-looking guy," my mother says on

the tape. "And he made me laugh." My mother worked in the payroll department and knew he took no deductions. "I figured he was single and available." She schemed with Joanie to let him know she was available, too.

"Miss Harris wants to go out with you," one of the secretaries told him.

My father thought it was a good idea. He came into the office looking for Miss Harris, but he didn't know Selma from Joanie. He tried Joanie.

"I think you want Selma," she said. Joanie was already dating the soap salesman she'd marry. "She's my sister."

Sid and Selma began to go out steadily, but they were not getting any closer to the altar.

"I'm through with marriage," my father had announced on their first date. He'd divorced his first wife after ten years; he found her living with someone else when he came back from the Navy.

"We'll take a week off, Selma, and go to Grossinger's," counseled Joanie, a tactician of postwar romance. "Then he'll realize how much he misses you."

"But what if he doesn't miss me?" my mother said.

"Don't worry so much, Selma."

Joanie and Selma went to Grossinger's. "She had a terrible time," Aunt Joanie told me. "She could only think of your father." But it worked. The day after she came back, he proposed.

Five months later they were married, and exactly

ten months after that I was born. Sandy toddled along right behind me.

My mother and father loved each other very much, but I don't believe theirs was a grand passion. They were mature and settled and happy to be married and parents. They rarely quarreled. They walked hand in hand. My graceless father, inelegant and insouciant, seemed to be my mother's dream guy. And because my mother left him alone in his orbit, she was his ideal wife.

My mother had wanted us to live in Green Acres. My father had wanted to stay in New York City. He didn't like suburbs, particularly ones whose civic credo was "to build the largest shopping center in Western Civilization." My mother listened to his objections and listened some more and they moved to Green Acres a year after I was born. She tolerated my father's occasional intransigence, his numerous idiosyncrasies, even the most ridiculous ones. Mine, she shortstopped with ease.

"I'm never using a spoon again," I declared at six, in the sweeping style of my father.

"Why not?" she asked.

"I don't believe in them."

"What *do* you believe in."

"Knives."

"Fine," she said, and served up a bowl of soup for dinner.

My mother was content to take care of home and family. Until I was nine my father worked in Port Jervis, often into the night. Sometimes he didn't come home until the weekend. On Saturday mornings I'd sneak into my parents' bedroom—I wanted to be reassured he was there.

One Saturday during first grade, I stood at the foot of their bed gazing at my father's sleeping figure. He slept in maroon silk pajamas from which his hairless, neon-white legs protruded. A subtle effluence of Vitalis filled the room. I gaped at the thatch of sleek black hair parted a little waywardly just above the left temple of his spectacles. My father sometimes fell asleep with his glasses on.

"Is anything wrong," my mother asked.

"No," I sputtered. "I just wanted a glass of water."

My mother instinctively understood my need to verify things. She defended my right to be a kid. She encouraged me to find out things for myself: to look under rocks for bugs, to get my knees skinned playing baseball, to write poetry even though I couldn't stop a sentence with a period.

My mother wanted nothing more than to be a model fifties housewife. She liked the steady efficiency of everyday life. She liked orderliness, believed that tomorrow would be pretty much like today. She put me to bed, woke me up, even helped me with my socks every morning. Yet my recollections of her can be hazy. I sometimes see her through a kind of filmy gauze, as I did when I was five and had asthma and spent half of kindergarten in an oxygen tent. The only sounds were my heart, my breath and the wheezing vaporizer. In this steamy enclosure, removed from the rest of the world, I pretended I was the King of Mars rocketing through the clouds of Venus. I talked with my co-pilot, my invisible companion, the King of Neptune. My mother would speak to me through the plastic curtain, her face indistinct beyond the foggy tent. She slipped her hand under the tent and held mine.

"That's not your real mother," said the invisible king.

"Sure it is," I said. "I know her voice."

"It could be one of your father's tapes."

"It isn't. It's her."

"How do you know?"

"I know." I knew my mother's hand by heart. My mother, the hand.

Mostly I remember her little rituals that punctuated my life. Each morning at breakfast she'd fire up a Parliament and let the ash curl into an arc and drop off as she talked to one of her girlfriends on the phone. Each night after dinner she made herself a Beefeater martini. Extra dry. Straight up. With an olive. Every Sunday she would fix me pancakes.

"Blueberry or buttermilk?" she'd ask. After mixing the ingredients into a wonderful, lumpy sludge, she poured the batter into the big, black iron skillet. I stood on a stool at the stove and waited for the batter to magically form the shapes of Looney Tunes characters with blueberries for the eyes and ears and mouths. I loved to watch Porky Pig sizzle and squeal.

I told her the bubbling batter looked like the craters of the moon.

"There's a reason for that," she said cryptically.

"You mean the moon is a pancake?"

She smiled, not the conspiratorial smile of my father, but a special smile she shared only with me. The first batch was buttery and honey-colored and crispy brown around the edges, and always mine.

When my mother went into the hospital for the first time, my father said she had a bad cold. While she was away nursing it, the prized orderliness of her home started coming apart. We had a maid to cook and clean, and my mother's sisters looked in on us now and then. Sandy loved the new attention. But I missed my mother's hand on my shoulders when she came in to shake me awake in the morning. I had to struggle to put on my socks myself. My father was a total washout as a pancake maker. His were hard and blackened and tasted like charcoal.

"Is the moon a big pancake?" I inquired at breakfast.

I remember the spikey glint in my father's eyes. He had an opportunity to deliver a lecture! When he got that look, I felt like I'd been orphaned.

"The real question is whether the moon originally was part of the earth or a small free planet," he began. I listened desultorily. "Here's some celestial food for thought—real gastronomical figures: Kepler's second law says the radius vector of a planet sweeps out equal areas in equal times. In other words, a planet's orbiting speed must be higher at the perihelion. The earth's top orbital speed is sixty-seven thousand, seven hundred and fifty miles an hour on January sixth when we're closest to the sun. The slowest at aphelion is sixty-five thousand, five hundred and twenty miles an hour."

"So," I said, after pondering this a while, "is the moon blueberry or buttermilk?"

"Better shut your flap, Jack."

For all my father's love of principles, axioms and logical thought, he prefered puns to conclusions. He hardly ever punished me. Not even for the time I locked Sally the maid in the closet.

I was teasing my sister. "You better behave, boy," Sally said. "Your mother's dying and you acting up."

"My mother's not dying!" I said, stunned.

"Why you think she's in the hospital?"

"She's sick. She has a bad cold."

"Who tell you that?"

"My father."

"Ever be in the hospital for a cold?"

"No."

"That's cause you ain't never been dying."

I didn't believe Sally. Not for a minute. Not for a second. What did she know about colds? But the fearful feeling that she was right oozed into my body like some terrible, greasy medicine. I hated her. When she stepped into the broom closet to put the vacuum cleaner away, I slammed the door shut.

By the time my father got home and let her out, she must have been in there an hour. "I quit," she snapped, and stamped out of the house.

"I locked her up," I said proudly. "She was a bad lady. She said Mommy's dying."

My father stared at me, sorting through what must have been an awful range of unsatisfactory responses. He said nothing. His shoulders sank. He slouched off to their bedroom and quietly shut the door. I waited for him to come out and tell me Sally was lying, that my mother wasn't dying, that she'd be home soon, putting everything in the house back in its proper place, sleeping again in their bedroom.

But he came out in a little while and made dinner and never mentioned what I'd done to Sally, or what she said. I didn't ask him anything, either. I was afraid to.

While my mother was in the hospital, my sister and my aunts could talk about hairdos and new school clothes, but I didn't speak their language, or my father's, either. I spent the summer in my room playing sockball, a solitary pleasure. I would grab a bunch of socks out of the top drawer of my father's bureau and tightly roll three or four into a resilient ball. Juggling the newly made sockball from hand to hand, I leapt around my bed, tossing it toward the goal, the triangular opening formed by the open door and a wall of my room. I became the first sockball All-American.

Sockball was suitable for lonely people in confined spaces—bedrooms, tollbooths, death-row cells. My first make-believe players took their names from the New York Knicks: Guerin, Sears, Braun. But soon I picked up names from words I heard my father use on the phone: Metastasis, Carcinoma, Sarcoma. I calculated their lifetime stats and knew what each of them looked like, who their wives were and how many children they had. Metastasis was tall, Carcinoma quick, Sarcoma powerful and deadly.

But I kept to my room mostly because my mother didn't want me to come see her in the hospital. When my father returned from his daily visit, Sandy and I would call her to say goodnight.

"When are you coming home?"

"The doctors say I'll be leaving real soon," she said cheerfully.

"So . . . how's your cold?"

"I'm doing much better. The doctors just have one or two more tests to run."

They must have been long tests because she stayed away about six weeks. When she got home, my father and my aunts kept telling her how good she looked. I didn't know what to say. She was shrunken and wizened, and had the splotchy yellow-brown look of a week-old lemon. She wore nightgowns and bathrobes around the house all day.

She told me I'd have to wake myself up now and put on my own socks. She quit cooking permanently. So my father turned out his black-edged pancakes every Sunday, like a burnt offering.

Chapter 3

The Minefield
of Sanity

"What's societize?" I asked my mother.

"I suppose it means to fit in like everybody else."

I could never imagine my uncles becoming societized. They had given up trying to fit in. Like cartoon characters jarred out of the square frame, they obeyed their own laws of gravity and physics. They trundled through the world on invisible tracks.

I realized this when I went to the hospital for my tonsilectomy. Half a dozen six-year-olds were lined up like loaves of bread in a bakery. The nurse gave us shots and told us to count backwards from a hundred. I was the last one. *Ninety-nine, ninety-eight, ninety-seven* . . . I watched the other kids nod off one by one. . . . *Seventy-seven, seventy-six, seventy-five* . . . Just me and one other kid were left, eyeing each other through the slats in our cribs. . . . *Fifty-nine, fifty-eight, fifty-seven* . . . Suddenly, Uncle Danny and Uncle Arthur appeared outside in the hall, dressed in duck suits and swinging from a trapeze. Uncle Arthur hung by his teeth from a slanting wire and slid down through burning hoops. Uncle Danny somersaulted from bar to bar, dangling by his heels. I watched slack-jawed from my bed while doctors, nurses, my parents went about their business beneath them, unaware of their amazing aerial act.

"Didn't you see Uncle Danny and Uncle Arthur fly?" I asked my father when I came to, tonsils out, throat sore.

"Fly?" He stared at me quizzically. "Oh!" he said. "That was just a hallucination brought on by the sodium pentothal, chemically speaking: C-eleven, H-seventeen, N-two, O-two . . ."

"Just tell me, Daddy," I squeaked. "I don't want to know why."

"No. They didn't fly. It's impossible."

But in my six-year-old heart I knew my uncles believed it *was* possible to fly. They were a constant rebuke to my father, who didn't trust his imagination enough to believe in his own irrationalities.

When Uncle Danny and Uncle Arthur came to dinner during my recuperation, my father offered a rhapsody about numbers for dessert: the mystery of zero, the meaning of pi, the topology of the infinite.

"There are only eight trustworthy people," Uncle Danny groaned unhappily. He looked sour, like the meal had disagreed with him.

"Huh?" said my father, blinking in surprise.

"There used to be twelve." Uncle Danny had a way with irrational numbers.

"What are you talking about?"

"Four died."

"Of what?"

"But eight are still alive."

"How'd you come up with that figure?"

"I have twenty-seven sources. Twenty-seven bona fide sources."

"Name one."

"Never!"

"Why not?"

"I took an oath."

My father never learned how to parry Uncle Danny's non-sequiturs. No matter how hard he tried to pin him, Uncle Danny would always slip away. It was a point of pride with Uncle Danny. My father used to say Uncle Danny was so stubborn that if he jumped off the Brooklyn Bridge, the police would find his body upriver. My father and Uncle Danny used to argue and argue and then argue some more. I'd hear their voices tumble together as they disparaged each other.

"You've buttered your bread," Uncle Danny shouted, "and now you've got to sleep in it."

"What the hell does that mean?"

"Let sleeping dogs lie, Sidney."

"On buttered bread?"

"It means what it means."

"It means nothing. It's meaningless. It's bullshit."

"And another thing, Sidney: Stop *breathing* in my cup!"

Finally, my exasperated father said, "Dan, you're just being abrasive."

Uncle Danny liked that. My father was right: He was abrasive. Uncle Danny was also acid and agitated and argumentative; bilious, bluff and briny; contentious and cantankerous; and on and on through honest and honorable; intractable and irksome; all the way to xenophobic, yeasty and zealous. I envied the way he could affect my father.

What distinguished Uncle Danny from his brothers was paranoia. "This is the country that persecuted Thomas Paine, the Rosenbergs and Jonas Salk," he'd say. "Why not me?" *They* were always after Uncle Danny. He could hear the goose steps.

Uncle Danny really believed all the world was a stage, and he was an unwilling player, a victim of some demonic director. He didn't have neighbors, only actors shuffling through a set designed by The Conspiracy. Their role was to disrupt him, keep him vulnerable and make him angry. Only his mother, Fannie, and Uncle Arthur and my father were real. He knew that was true because The Conspiracy had already overcome Uncle Leo and Uncle Harry and secreted them in madhouses.

Uncle Danny's paranoia was continually confirmed: At one time he worked as a house painter and a sadistic electrician crept up behind him and touched two high-voltage wires to the base of his neck. My father said that was why Uncle Danny's tongue drooped over his lower lip, and why he sometimes panted like a dog. After the run-in with the electrician, Uncle Danny was never again comfortable with technological expertise. He particularly distrusted my father's. He acquired the wary, drained alertness of the point man in an infantry squad, tiptoeing through the minefield of sanity.

Uncle Danny charmed me. Under his tutelage, I heard *Mary Had a Little Lamb* and thought "its fleas were white as snow." When I was five, he introduced me to the Toe Collector, the man in the booth at the entrance to the Holland Tunnel.

"Give the Toe Collector a quarter," he'd chortle. For years I feared that my parents would forget their wallets and we'd have to fork over our toes.

My mother had no more patience for Uncle Danny's games than did my father. If Uncle Danny made my father angry, he reduced my mother to a state of hand-wringing desperation. On the night Uncle Danny was on our patio refusing to break his oath, my mother was in the kitchen preparing meatballs and spaghetti. At dinner, Uncle Danny took one bite and suddenly shot straight up in his chair with a harsh, sputtering gurgle, then collapsed, choking.

"What's wrong?" asked my father, slapping him on the back.

"It's the food!"

"What about it?"

"It's contaminated. Selma's trying to kill me!"

Uncle Danny had watched my mother make the sauce and got the notion oregano was toxic. My mother swallowed her anger and offered him another plate. Uncle Danny refused it. Finally, Uncle Arthur washed the sauce off the spaghetti and Uncle Danny ate it. My mother might well have wanted to kill him then.

Uncle Arthur, too, could pull a few screws from my parents' hinges, though he undermined them not with guile but with innocence.

He arrives in this memory hauling onto our doorstep a grocery cart jammed with dog-eared comic books, sprung toasters and Hebrew bank calendars. He reaches into a cardboard box tied with shoelaces and passes Uncle Danny a phonograph record. "It's a seventy-nine," Uncle Arthur says proudly.

"What do you mean, seventy-nine?" says my father.

"Seventy-nine. It's on the label."

"Listen, Arthur: Records are thirty-three, forty-five and seventy-eight. Once in a while, sixteen-and-a-half. Maybe."

"This one's a seventy-nine."

"It's faster," says Uncle Danny.

"I'm telling you, records don't go faster than seventy-eight."

"This one's a seventy-nine," repeats Uncle Arthur.

"The turntable determines the speed, not the record."

"Maybe where you come from, Sidney," scoffs Uncle Danny.

My mother looks at the label.

"It's a seventy-eight RPM. It cost seventy-nine *cents*!"

She puts down the record and starts to laugh. Uncle Arthur joins in. And finally even my father and Uncle Danny, the principal combatants.

Normally, my mother wasn't so tolerant of Uncle Arthur's quirks. She judged him a defective role model.

He was never too discriminating about the junk he collected. Except for shoelaces. He didn't collect just any old shoelaces. He carefully removed the long, fettucini-shaped ones from the old sneakers. Over the years he filled dozens of shopping bags with them.

"You'd be surprised at all the colors they come in," he told me.

I was.

"Green, blue, red. . . ." he said. "I haven't seen many yellows."

When I was six, my father took me to see the ice skaters in Rockefeller Center. We got off the F Train at Fiftieth Street only to see a gaunt, familiar figure, two grubby sneakers draped around his neck, rifling through a trash bin by the turnstiles.

"Arthur!" yelped my father, embarrassed for his brother, his son, but mostly for himself.

Sure enough, Uncle Arthur was on a scavenger hunt. He was stalking P. F. Flyers in gutters, nicking Keds from Dumpsters and rescuing Converse Hi-Tops from incinerators. He saved the laces the way elephant hunters saved tusks. I'd have gladly joined his shoelace safaris. When Miss Clarke made us write a composition about one of our relatives, most of my classmates chose grandparents. I picked Uncle Arthur.

"My Uncle Arthur is a scavenger hunter," I wrote. "He wears yesterdays clothes and brings me stuff that looks like garbage. Some is real neat and some is already broke."

Now *I* pick through the past for the stuff of memories, and I have to do my own scavenging.

Uncle Arthur's habitual hoarding dovetailed nicely with Uncle Danny's paranoia. They lived together in the Bronx, where they'd moved in the early 1930s with Fannie and Uncle Leo. By the time I made my first visit, in 1959, my grandmother was dead and Uncle Leo daft. It was my eighth birthday.

My mother's present to me was a trip to a Yankees game with two friends.

"Any two friends?" I asked.

"Sure."

"Okay," I said. "Uncle Danny and Uncle Arthur."

I couldn't think of anybody I'd rather go to a ball game with, but my mother and Uncle Danny barely spoke. He considered her an interloper who had spirited my father away. He had tried to prevent their marriage. My father told me Uncle Danny even wanted to sit in on their dates. Danny, the oldest brother, perceived himself as the patriarch of the family, dedicated to protecting his brothers from matrimony. He detested women. He wouldn't watch a horse race if a filly was running.

"They don't even like baseball," my mother protested.

I appealed to my father. He offered a diversion:
He'd take me camping anywhere in New York.

"Anywhere?"

"Yeah."

"Okay," I said. "How about Danny and Arthur's
apartment?"

My father shrugged.

"It's his birthday," he told my mother. "He's entitled."

My mother balked. She had visited Danny and
Arthur's apartment just once.

"It's a junk museum," she said. "They're pack
rats."

"They're more like Tasmanian fillaloo rodents,"
corrected my father, never passing up a chance for
instruction. "They can crawl into a hole and pull in
the hole after them."

"I don't want them to pull my son into their
hole!"

The image of the fillaloo rodent only piqued my
interest in seeing Uncle Danny and Uncle Arthur's
apartment for myself. My mother's reaction reminded me of what my father had told me about
the Collyer brothers, those celebrated Hermits of
Harlem. He didn't believe in fairy tales, so he
served up real-life grotesqueries.

I would listen raptly to his stories about the junk-
jammed mansion where the blind and bedridden
Homer Collyer lived with his devoted younger

brother, Langley. My father described how Langley nursed Homer, washed him, fed him a hundred oranges a week in a bizarre attempt to cure his blindness, and saved newspapers for him to read when he regained his sight. Fifty-seven years of newspapers. Langley, my father recounted, was buried in an avalanche of rubbish when he tripped one of the booby traps he had set against burglars. I knew all the details: how Homer starved to death, how Langley's body had been gnawed by rats, how the police had searched the city for Langley while he lay dead beneath the debris in his own house.

Sensational bedtime stories, I thought. They filled the dark with nightmares, chimeras, bogeymen. To me, Uncle Danny and Uncle Arthur *were* Homer and Langley, an impression my mother reinforced by referring to them as "your father's cockamamie Collyer brothers."

Since Fannie's death six years earlier, Uncle Danny and Uncle Arthur had lived in seclusion. My mother said they never invited anyone to their apartment. She made it sound haunted, dirty, overrun with rats. It sounded like Dracula's castle to me. I became convinced they stacked dead bodies in the foyer. The more she demurred, the more I insisted. I was mad at her, anyway.

It had started with my sideburns. I'd looked in the mirror one morning and decided I hated them. I kept evening them up with my father's razor until they disappeared.

"You look like a screwball," she said.

"What's a screwball?"

"Your Uncle Danny."

She drew in sideburns with eyebrow pencil and sent me to school.

"Why do you have black lines next to your ears?" asked Dicky Haas.

"My mother put them on."

"What for?"

"I cut off my sideburns."

"You look like a screwball."

I tried to pull my collar up over my ears for the next two weeks.

My mother went back in the hospital and I got madder. She left us for a month this time and I felt she owed me something special for my birthday.

"I want to go camping with Uncle Danny and Uncle Arthur. I'm entitled."

"Me too," said Sandy.

"No way! It's *my* birthday."

"If you want to stay with your uncles," said my mother, "you'll have to take along your sister."

"She can come," I said grudgingly, "but she can't sit next to me."

We waited for Uncle Danny's weekly phone call. He would call collect from a different phone booth every Sunday, a premature G. Gordon Liddy who feared The Conspiracy. He'd whisper the number into the receiver and we'd have to phone him back. That way, his calls couldn't be traced.

The call came. We called back. My father put me on.

"Can I sleep over next Saturday?" I asked.

"Ask Arthur," he said. I imagined Uncle Arthur crowded into the phone booth with him. I asked. Uncle Arthur answered with a characteristic pause.

"Well . . ." he said uncertainly. He paused. Silence. "Sure."

"Make them promise to clean up," my mother urged my father.

"Well . . ." said Uncle Arthur. "Okay."

"Can I go to the ball game, too?" I asked.

"Why not?" sighed my mother. "You're entitled."

The day of the game I woke up to see my father standing over me in his bathrobe.

"You awake?" he asked.

"I am," I said, bolting upright.

"Your mother's feeling sick today. Why don't you get some more sleep and we'll watch the game on TV."

"What!" I said, panicked. "I told everybody in school I was going."

"Her cold might get worse."

"Can't she take some pills?"

He shook his head.

"Come on, you promised."

Yes, he admitted, he had promised, but he proposed instead to take us all to the circus next week, when my mother was feeling better. Sandy, who was standing by the door, said, "Cool!" and my father seemed satisfied.

"No, it's not cool," I whined as my father left. I

got out of bed and darted for the door to his bed-room. "You promised we could go," I said. "You *promised*." He didn't answer. My sister was sitting on her bed, singing, "We're going to the circus, we're going to the circus."

I broke for Sandy's room, ready to strangle her. Just as I was about to become an only child, my mother called in to announce she was well enough to go to the game after all.

"Don't worry, Mommy," I said. "I'll bring extra Kleenex."

My father drove the Chevy. As always, I'd tally the cars he passed along Sunrise Highway, and the ones that passed him. Few did: He drove as if he were in the last lap of the Indy 500 time trials with an hour to make up.

I'd present him with running totals. He taught me to use a slide rule to figure out his average.

"It'll help you with your math," he explained.

Tiring of counting cars, I nudged Sandy. "Look," I said, "there's a hippopotamus."

"Where?"

"Back there."

"I don't see it."

"You missed it. And the elephants, too."

"Mommy, was there *really* a hippo?"

Bringing Sandy along wasn't acceptable. She was a six-year-old girl, a dopey little sister interchangea-ble with everyone else's dopey little sister who would rather go to a circus than a ball game. She was constantly crying and running to my mother with hurt feelings. Stupid things made her happy, like wearing a party dress and hearing an adult tell her she looked pretty, tittering and tattling with her girlfriends, and stumbling around in my mother's high heels. And I had to put up with her. Even at Yankee Stadium, on my birthday.

At first, waiting at the gate to the grandstands for Uncle Danny and Uncle Arthur, anything seemed possible, even that I'd catch a fly ball. But the possibilities diminished as we waited. We missed batting practice. We heard the National Anthem echo out of the stands. My feet yearned to move. My heart worried about missing Bob Turley striking out the first batter of a perfect game. I prayed my two weird uncles could find the ballpark.

They materialized just before the first pitch. Uncle Arthur had made Uncle Danny walk the thirty-seven blocks to the stadium: He wouldn't spring for the fifteen-cent subway fare. "It's a waste of money," he said.

My mother sighed in disbelief. My father snapped a picture of the three of us. I've still got it. Uncle Danny's wearing a brown suit, a brown vest, a white shirt, a brown brocade tie, brown wingtips and a brown fedora with a yarmulke underneath so he would never be bare-headed before the Lord.

Uncle Arthur looked about the same as he does now. His splintery features and graying stubble gave him the air of an old man on the skids. His hair and whiskers were cut at the same length, about a week's growth. He trimmed all hairs himself. Uncle

Arthur's tortoiseshell glasses were so wadded with black electrical tape that his ears bugged out. He carried his daily cache of newspapers rolled under his arm.

"Is Uncle Arthur a scarecrow, Mommy?" asked my sister, then ducked behind her.

Uncle Arthur opened his windbreaker to reveal five more layers of clothing—an inner jacket, a sweater, a jersey and two pairs of long woolen underwear. "I'm a walking radiator," he said giddily.

Even before sitting down, Uncle Danny, the old Socialist whose roots went back to Gene Debs, looked around for government infiltrators. Who sent the peanut vendor down our aisle? What was in the hot dog he had to pass along our row? Why had the fat man in the black angora sweater been planted behind him?

Uncle Danny looked with disdain at Mickey Mantle in the batter's box. From our seats in the upper deck, The Mick looked very small. He pulled a foul ball up into our section. I strained toward it with the sweet dread I might drop it.

Uncle Danny was genuinely terrified. He curled up in his seat.

Mantle hit a high, arching pop foul that seemed to hang over our heads. I ran into the aisle like a disoriented left-fielder. The ball dropped thirty feet away.

When I got back to our row, Uncle Danny was still cowering—beneath his seat this time.

"What's wrong?" I asked.

"See that number seven?" he said. "See him look up here? He spotted me. See those balls come up? You think he's a ballplayer? He's trying to get me."

"Mickey Mantle? Does he know you, Uncle Danny?"

"Know me? He's trying to *kill* me!"

"Mantle, Uncle Danny? He's trying to hit a home run."

Mantle dodged an inside pitch. "Kill him, Mickey," yelled the furry fat man.

"See? *See?*" Uncle Danny bent down and whispered. I felt his breath damp against my face. "They're in cahoots."

My mother, a big Yankees fan, cheered with every pitch. "Throw your screwball," she yelled at the Yankee pitcher.

"But you said Uncle Danny's a screwball," I said. My mother raised a finger across her lips, shushing me.

My engineer father leafed through a *Scientific American* between batters, putting it down during the seventh-inning stretch to discourse on Bernoulli's principle.

"Which, of course," he said, "governs the behavior of baseballs in flight." I had made the mistake of asking why a curveball curves.

Uncle Arthur sat motionless, demonstrating the Second Law of Thermodynamics.

"Arthur once broke his nose playing ball," said my father.

"Did you, Uncle Arthur?"

"No, but my mother did. She broke my nose."

When Uncle Arthur was small, he slept next to Fannie, who kept a bat under the bed. He awoke one morning on the floor with a bloody schnoz. Fannie had had a dream of fastballs. She grabbed the bat in her sleep and lined Arthur's head to center for a base hit. It was a famous family story.

In contrast to Uncle Arthur's comatose attendance, Uncle Danny was generating enough nervous energy to light the stadium. He jumped like a bug in a jar. He screamed. He cackled. He chattered at the players from his seat. His fingers twitched and wriggled, his elbows sliced the air, his hands spun on their wrists like loosely mounted propellors.

The game came apart in the top of the eleventh inning. For the Yankees, for my uncles, for me. Baltimore rallied. Single. Double. Single. Walk. Yankee manager Casey Stengel slouched to the mound looking like Uncle Arthur searching for shoelaces.

My scorecard ends there. Out of the late afternoon chatter rose the small, sad, incongruous sound of Uncle Danny, faintly, faintly singing the "Internationale."

"Can it, you goddamn Red," bellowed the fat government infiltrator behind him.

"Trotskyite tool of The Conspiracy!" Uncle Danny retorted.

"For Chrissake, Danny," my mother interjected, "we're at a baseball game."

"Whore of Babylon!" grumbled Uncle Danny.

"Watch your mouth, Dan," cautioned my father, turning a page of his *Scientific American*.

"You made us bring them, Sid," sniped my mother.

"Go back to Russia," blared the fat man.

"McCarthyite!" shrieked my mother.

"Jerk!" sniffed my father, glancing up.

"I have to go to the toilet," Sandy cried.

Uncle Arthur retreated further into catatonia.

"Look at them," Uncle Danny said, pointing at Stengel and the players on the mound. "Plotting. Pogrom. Cossacks, cossacks, cossacks . . ."

"Shut up, you abrasive bastard," my father demanded.

Uncle Danny cupped his hands over his ears. "Red-Baiter!"

"That's it, Sid," my mother said. "His birthday's wrecked. Let's go." She got up and started walking out. We could only follow. Me, miserably. It didn't matter—the Yanks were losing, anyway.

My mother liked the idea of me staying over at my uncles' less and less. Working up a few tears, I reminded her I didn't even get to see the end of the game. She relented. Now, Uncle Danny wouldn't get in the car with her. "God, Sid, let's all go on the subway," she said. "We'll get the car later."

Uncle Arthur blanched. "It's a waste of money."

"Jesus, Arthur," said my father. "Selma just got out of the hospital."

My mother came up with the change.

We were a straggly procession. My father strode

out in front with the hip-swiveling stride he prac-
ticed so that he could walk faster than anyone else.
Uncle Danny followed with quick mincing steps.
Sandy and my mother trailed behind.

I saw my mother stop halfway up the steps to the
station to take big gulping breaths. "Come *on,*
Mommy," Sandy said impatiently. "You're too slow."
My mother looked at me: I turned the other way,
toward Uncle Arthur, who was scraping along with
his head down, peering intently into the corners of
the steps. Now and then he'd bend over to pick
something up—a shoe, a penny, a bent can.

"What are you doing, Uncle Arthur?"

"Collecting," he said.

The cavalcade of Lidzes stopped at last on the
platform. The subway was full of pushy, noisy people who didn't look like anybody I'd seen in Green
Acres. "Actors," confided Uncle Danny. "Actors, every one."

Chapter 4

The Temple of Junk

By the time we reached my uncles' apartment, my mother looked as if she was about to say no again.

"What about your asthma?" she said.

I shrugged. I was now a street kid: I had been on the subway.

Uncle Danny and Uncle Arthur lived in a grimy brick-and-brownstone apartment house, a rectangle of streaked blackness set against the lighter adjoining buildings. The lobby was long, narrow, and dark. We walked past a row of mailboxes.

"See?" whispered Uncle Danny.

"See what?" I whispered back.

Uncle Danny nodded toward the boxes. The Conspirators had stuffed them with letters to make him believe that people actually lived in the place. But Uncle Danny knew they were only props.

"You can't come up," Uncle Danny told my parents.

"Of course we're coming up," said my mother.

"No," said Uncle Danny.

"No," said Uncle Arthur.

"Jesus Christ," my father exploded. "I'm your brother."

"Okay," Uncle Danny said. "You come up, Sidney. Just for a minute. But you can't bring Selma."

"I wouldn't step foot in that filthy sty, Danny," said my mother, stung. "If you want my kids to stay there, Sid, you'd better check the beds, check the bathroom, check the food. Look for rats. Look for roaches. See if they washed the dishes this year. Find out where they've hidden the corpses." She handed me the little bag with our pajamas and toothbrushes.

My father lifted Sandy on his shoulders and took my hand. We climbed the big marble steps to the second-floor apartment. Uncle Arthur disappeared into the darkness. He tinkered with locks. I could see the living room was barricaded with wire netting, and behind the netting, milk crates, tin cans and barrels were piled to the ceiling. I was sure my father would make us leave. My sister started screaming, "I want to go home!" My father was about to carry her downstairs when she changed her mind. "I want to stay," she pleaded. My father put her down, barely looking at the apartment. He knew what was in there and he probably thought we needed a little exposure to the gritty side of life. He gave us each our good-bye kiss and took off down the stairs.

I leaned against the door, and it swung open. I didn't see any dead bodies. Yet.

As soon as Sandy looked into the shadows of the

junk-filled room, she began to blubber again. Uncle Danny picked her up and rocked her in his arms. He sang her a verse of the Daffy Duck song in his creaky, pseudocantorial voice:

> Oh, when they say I'm nutsy
> It sure gives me a pain,
> Please pass the ketchup
> I think it's going to rain.

Uncle Arthur led us in. The tangled rooms had the heavy atmosphere of long-sealed Egyptian tombs, like the ones in *The Mummy*. Towers of cereal cartons and soap boxes honeycombed the living room and spread into the kitchen. We trailed him through hills of newspapers, mounds and mounds of tightly packed newspapers, all carefully tied with cord. They stank of mildew and decay.

"Why do you collect all these newspaper?" I asked Uncle Arthur.

Uncle Arthur tilted his head and looked at me curiously from slitted eyes. "I don't collect them."

"Then why do you have so many?"

"I've been busy. I haven't had time to read them."

Uncle Arthur's papers closed around us like a dark forest. Moving through them was like touring his brain. Without him for a guide, you ran the risk of tripping one of his Collyer-like booby traps patched together from frayed rope, jam jars and gum wrappers. Or simply getting lost in the dimension of junk.

70   *Franz Lidz*

Uncle Arthur beamed proudly at the chaos. "People throw away a lot of things that are good," he said.

I saw broken brooms, dusty books, rakes, baby carriages, moldy carpets, coffee grinders, saw horses, umbrellas, frying pans, a grandfather clock with no face, tooth pullers—all sorts of stuff that Uncle Arthur had lugged in from the streets. A calendar girl. Seventy-nines stacked like pancakes. Bushel baskets brimming with empty packs of Lucky Strikes. Grocery bags stuffed with twigs, bottle caps, swizzle sticks.

Uncle Arthur's ball collection rivaled his shoelace collection for greatness. He was one of the last practitioners of the arcane art of ball-fishing. After a heavy rain, he'd station himself where a deep concrete spillway—it had to be at least fifty feet wide—opened into the Harlem River. His ball trap was a coat hanger fashioned into a spiral and tied on a long piece of string. Casting it into the swollen waters with the finesse of a trout fisherman on the Beaver Kill, he pulled in punchballs, footballs, soccer balls. The Lost Balls of the Bronx, washed by rainwater down gutters and through sewer traps toward the sea, were intercepted and saved by Uncle Arthur.

Uncle Arthur learned this skill from his father, Simon, whom he had watched fish for bananas on the Lower East Side near Pier Forty-two, where the stevedores unloaded fruit. Now and then a bunch or even a hand of bananas would fall overboard. Si-

mon, the sly old patriarch, hooked them with a
stone tied to the end of a string, gingerly hoisted
them from the murky brown water of the East
River, and brought them home.

Uncle Arthur told me he had abandoned banana
collecting.

"After a couple of weeks they start stinking up
the apartment," he said.

Occasionally he'd exchange some balls for tin
cans or empty soda bottles, more negotiable currency in the junk trade. "Years ago I could get six
soda bottles for a tennis ball," Uncle Arthur la-
mented. "Today nobody has soda bottles. I can't get
nothing." But Uncle Arthur never threw away anything. The balls just sat—inert and bounceless
surplus.

He was a creature of simple needs, Uncle Arthur. He found his clothes in the street. He never
turned on more than two lights at a time, and
searched for replacement bulbs in abandoned
buildings. He washed wax paper for reuse.

"I've almost eliminated the use of money," he
said with a smile of satisfaction.

Uncle Danny's voice filtered through the junk.
He was still singing to Sandy.

> Oh, you can't bounce a meatball
> Though try with all your might,
> Turn on the radio
> I want to fly a kite.

Sandy finally stopped crying.

Uncle Arthur and I delved through dim arteries and endless secret shafts. His paper fortress was better than any tree house, an enclosed, airless world, askew and disorienting as passageways in a funhouse.

"Where are we going, Uncle Arthur?"

He was a dark presence beside me. I held his hand. It was soft and leathery, like my baseball glove—not at all like my father's firm and muscular grasp. Suddenly, I was afraid. "Nobody knows where they're going," Uncle Arthur began. He was in an uncharacteristically verbose mood. "A little patience. You need a little patience. You remind me of Sidney when he was little. He always wanted to go someplace very fast. He was a wild boy. You know where the fast ones get to? They get to be dead first."

He pulled my arm up against him: My hand started to go numb. He kept talking. "You know he taught me how to read, your father, how to write? I was the slow one. You know I hitchhiked back from a farm in Massachusetts? They taught me how to milk a cow there. I had a job milking a cow. One day they beat me up and fired me. But I could still milk a cow if I had to."

I listened to Uncle Arthur's slow, halting cadences. I wondered what he meant. The darkness tightened around us. I wondered if I could milk a cow. I wondered if Uncle Arthur was crazy.

I slipped my hand away. "Come on, Uncle Arthur. Come on."

But Uncle Arthur wanted to talk. And he did, in a way I hadn't heard till then. I guess he felt safe standing inside his newspaper fortress. "My first job was leading a blind man. He sold combs, toothbrushes, shoelaces. We'd get on the train to Hoboken and I'd take him to every bar in town. I'd say, 'He's my father.' If a fight started, I'd look for change in the gutter outside the bar. Whatever I found, the blind man made me give him half. Sometimes the blind man took me on trips. We'd go to the colored sections so he could spend his money. He'd pay to get in bed with a colored woman. I'd stay on the side."

"Of the bed?" I asked. I didn't understand this story.

"No, a chair. In a corner. By the door.

"He paid her combs and toothbrushes, I think. I don't know. What the hell. He was cheap. He used to keep me late hours. Never paid me overtime. Cheap, cheap, cheap. I got angry so I stole shoelaces from him. Maybe that's how I started collecting."

I wanted to be somewhere else. I wanted to be with my sister. I wanted to be with Uncle Danny, even if he was crazy, too. Then Uncle Arthur said: "You need to learn patience. A person needs patience to collect. If I didn't have patience, I'd be in a nuthouse. You think it's easy to catch a ball in the water?"

At last he led me through an arch of cereal cartons and we came upon Uncle Danny and Sandy. Uncle Danny had stopped singing. He was making dinner on a kerosene stove.

He and Uncle Arthur cooked and ate in a small grotto among the stacks in the living room. Uncle Danny had set Sandy on a pile of papers before a table covered with more papers. She sat there swinging her legs as if she were ready to take off running.

"What do you want?" Uncle Danny asked.

"Cheeseburgers," Sandy and I chorused.

"Coming right up," said Uncle Danny. He bushwacked his way back to the kerosene stove and brought us plates of chicken. The alleged bird seemed to have been boiling on the stove since the end of the New Deal. A kosher chicken. Uncle Danny had to see it killed right in front of him in the Orthodox way. He was a strictly observant Jew who hewed closely to the laws of the Old Testament. He prayed morning and night. He went to shul every Saturday. Uncle Arthur reluctantly tagged along.

Uncle Danny said the blessing before the meal. *"Baruch ata adonai elohainu melech ha-olam . . ."*

Sandy and I glanced at each other. We had never heard the prayer before. Our father didn't allow grace at our table. We listened, my sister and I, mystified by the ancient Hebrew words filling the candlelit darkness in this strange tabernacle of junk.

". . . *she-hakol nee-yeh bidvaro.*" He swayed as he prayed and he finished with a long, hollow, lamenting oo-o-o-o. He asked me what kind of tea I wanted, not that it mattered. They used the same teabags over and over.

"Chamomile," I said, playing along. It was the only tea I'd ever heard of. Peter Rabbit got it when he was sick and I'd always wanted to try some, but my mother told me I was too young.

Uncle Danny handed me a well-used Tetley tea bag. I watched my uncles closely. Uncle Danny put his bag in his spoon, wrapped the string around it and pulled. Uncle Arthur squeezed his against the side of the cup. I tried to wrap mine around my spoon, but the bag broke and all the leaves floated in the water.

The tea was tasteless anyway. Just like the chicken, which was gray and stringy and fell apart on my fork. Hairs stuck out of the skin.

"Why did you ask for chicken if you're not eating it?" asked Danny accusingly.

"I didn't!"

"Didn't what?"

"I'm not hungry, I guess," I said with resignation.

My uncles and their apartment were losing their glamour.

"Let's go to the sitting room," said Uncle Danny. "We have presents for you." I'd never heard of a sitting room, and God knows where Uncle Danny got the idea from. Uncle Arthur led us through a hole punched through a wall of papers. Of course, there was no place to sit. Uncle Danny plopped onto a ledge of more papers, and I plopped onto his lap.

Uncle Arthur yanked a checkerboard from a column of phone books. "Thanks!" I said. "I play every week with Mrs. Kauffman."

She was the child psychologist my mother had hired to determine if my asthma was psychosomatic. Mrs. Kauffman and I sat around a board, playing almost all the way through our half-hour sessions. I liked checkers. Uncle Arthur had taught me and we were evenly matched. But when I played Mrs. Kauffman, she mostly asked questions.

"What questions?" asked Uncle Arthur.

"She wants to know what games I play with my . . ."

"Peeny?" demanded Uncle Danny.

"Uh-huh."

"Tell her nothing!" he shouted, rising to his feet so quickly that I fell out of his lap. "Nothing, nothing, nothing! She's a manipulator."

I thought of Mrs. Kauffman. She was a neatly coiffed woman with a bright smile who wore big round glasses and a strand of pearls. She looked like the ladies Nanny Ruth sat next to at Hadassah luncheons. But Uncle Danny was right, I decided. There *was* something wrong with Mrs. Kauffman. She never won at checkers. Even when I blundered and she should have pounced, she still lost.

"Don't play the game," said Uncle Danny. He had a point. She couldn't lose if I didn't win. I took his advice the next time I went to see Mrs. Kauffman.

I set up a triple jump, which she pretended not to see. I refused to move. We just sat there, she not winning, me not losing—the perfect application of Uncle Danny's philosophy. I told my mother I didn't want to go any more, and there were no more sessions with Mrs. Kauffman.

"Arthur!" said Uncle Danny. "Give him a high-bouncer."

Uncle Arthur jerked me up from the floor, then reached into his box of found balls and produced a Spaldeen. I bounced it off the living room wall. Nobody told me to stop. I hadn't played ball in our living room in Green Acres since my mother installed a white shag rug and banished everyone with feet.

"I want one, too," Sandy said. Uncle Arthur gave her a golf ball.

Next Uncle Danny sorted through a tin of Uncle Arthur's buttons and took out a scarab, a small glistening chunk of feldspar incised with a crocodile and an ibis, as supple as smoke.

"Jewish slaves made this thousands of years ago for the Pharaohs of Egypt," Uncle Danny said. "The Sultan of Muscat coveted it. Emperors fought and killed for it."

He explained that the ancient Egyptians took the scarab design from the dung beetle. "A wonderfully useful insect," he said. "It rolls elephant dung into balls to attract lady beetles." Uncle Danny had the same didactic streak as my father, only he favored fantasy over reality.

"What's elephant dung?" asked Sandy, breaking the spell.

"Doo-doo," said Uncle Arthur. "Big elephant doo-doo."

"The Egyptians saw the beetles roll the dung across the sandy desert floor," Uncle Danny told us. He loved to say the words *Egyptians, Pharaohs*. In the mysterious half-dark of this strange apartment, he intoned the words like a warning.

"The Pharaohs carved the scarab to look like the beetle. In the beetle, they saw the sun, the moon, the flow of life. They thought it created itself from the ball that kept rolling, rolling, rolling . . ."

He put it in my hand.

"Treasure this. Keep it. It is powerful."

I cherished the scarab and have it to this day.

That evening Uncle Danny told stories nonstop for three hours, pausing only to cut slivers of birthday cake and pour more thin tea. I sat in Uncle Danny's lap, Sandy in Uncle Arthur's. I remember Uncle Danny looking toward the windows a lot. Which now strikes me as odd. They were painted over in the same lizard color as the walls, or maybe they had just never been washed. Nobody ever opened them. Uncle Danny didn't want prying eyes.

Uncle Danny pulled a photo down from the wall. He and my father during the war. My father smiles broadly from beneath his sailor's cap. Uncle Danny wears Army ODs and the faintest of skeptical smiles.

"You look handsome," said Sandy.

"I was also brave," said Uncle Danny.

He quit work at his uncles' wallpaper store in Brooklyn during the summer of 1942 to enlist. He was not quite thirty-nine. He went into the Army as a private. He was a proud, vigorous Socialist. He was eager to fight the Nazis. "A quartermaster, they made me," he said. "A quartermaster! The nerve! The gall! For two years I supplied food and medicine."

Uncle Danny rattled off his campaigns: "Naples, Rome, Arno, Foggia, Normandy. They gave me a good conduct medal. Who the hell were they to judge my behavior?" He made corporal before he came home, but he never sewed the stripes on.

Uncle Danny propelled his tale with grimace and gesture and wink and nod and growl and groan. "I went back to work for my uncles. Borowitz Paint and Wallpaper. In two weeks they called me in and asked, 'Can you sell?'

"Can I sell? Sure, I say. My Uncle Jimmy gave me two suitcases: 'Make up your own route.' I walked all over Canal Street with my two suitcases. Samples. Wallpaper samples.

"Walked! You're damned well right I walked. For fifteen dollars a week. With two suitcases. On Monday to the Battery. Tuesday to Fourteenth Street. Wednesday, Hell's Kitchen. Then Thursday was Washington Heights. I went into the side streets. Wherever I saw a little store.

"And every store I went into wanted wallpaper,

wallpaper. Everybody wanted wallpaper. This is a helluva business to go into, I thought."

So Uncle Danny used his mustering-out pay to open a wallpaper store in White Plains. He ran the business on the theory that customers might occasionally be right, but so what? He treated them with complete tyranny, tossed them out with utter impartiality. His roar could have been his motto.

"People came in. Crooks. Shysters. 'Can I see this blue floral pattern in red?'

"I'd say, 'What's wrong with blue?' I'd say, 'Nothing's wrong with blue. I don't need your opinion.' I'd say, 'I don't need your business. Get out of my store. Get *out*! O-U-T.' "

Uncle Danny didn't have the temperament to be a shopkeeper. He was far better suited to being an annalist, and was the keeper of the family lore. Much of what I know about my family comes from him. My father, who could recite the periodic table, didn't know a second cousin from a second baseman. But Uncle Danny remembered everything—the weddings, the births, the illnesses, the tragedies, the innuendo and the indiscretions. He invested the most trivial event with a peculiar and personal immediacy. The people in his stories seemed to be controlled by mysterious and unfathomable forces that showed themselves through sudden cataclysmic shifts of fortune.

Uncle Danny narrated Lidz history like a rabbi reading from the Book of Kings: "And Sheemon begat Hesh, and Hesh begat Simon, and Simon begat

Danny and Leo and Harry and Arthur and Sidney, and Sidney begat . . ." His voice was clear, direct, uncolored.

"Eighteen sixty-six. Simon Lidz was born September twelfth, eighteen sixty-six."

"Was he a good guy or a bad guy," I asked.

"He was my father, your grandfather."

In Uncle Danny's stories, women were miserable, men spiteful, relatives miserably spiteful.

"A one-room apartment we lived in," he said. "No plumbing. Cold-water house. Cockroaches. Lice. Big rats galore. Crowded. The only heat was from the kitchen stove. People lived cheap back then. Papa lived on pennies from teaching English. Pennies! Everything was pennies. P-E-N-N-I-E-S."

Uncle Danny spoke in staccato bursts, as if the story had been told too often and someone was going to make him shut up. "You couldn't even take a bath at home. Had to go to the public bath. Two cents. Give you about four minutes. They'd bang on the door if you didn't get out. Bang on the door and drag you out.

"Or you went to the bud, the Yiddish bath. Strictly steam. Stone slabs like steps. The higher you went, the hotter it was."

Uncle Danny said Simon once broke through a window on ladies' night.

"Why did he do that?"

"For ventilation."

The ladies said Simon was peeping.

"Damned miserable women tried to get him arrested!" my disbelieving uncle said. "Tried to put him in jail. Jail!"

"J-A-I-L," I said.

Uncle Danny fit a lot of words into a minute; there were enough stories for a lifetime of birthdays. Tender and bitter and funny and tedious, he showed no signs of tiring. Neither did Sandy. Even Uncle Arthur seemed mildly interested in this outpouring of Lidziana.

Uncle Danny jostled me aside and reached for a basin of water on the floor. He took off his shoes and soaked his feet. He worked very, very carefully on his soles. When you're a messenger and your younger brother won't let you take the subway, it's important to take care of your feet. And Uncle Danny had walked thirty-seven blocks to Yankee Stadium that afternoon.

"Nineteen oh-six," Uncle Danny said, resuming the geneology. "Papa left the button factory in nineteen oh-six. Opened the Lidz International Shrinking Company."

Uncle Danny told me you could still see some of the traces of the sign Simon had painted on the Lower East Side building. He said he could make out the faded *L* gilded on the brick, half hidden beneath newer signs. Nevertheless, Uncle Danny assured me that even if I couldn't find the golden *L*, I'd have no trouble locating the family motto painted between the second- and third-story windows: "We Shrink to Expand."

"What did he shrink?" I asked.

"Remnants, piece goods."

I nodded dumbly.

"You know tapestry?" said Uncle Arthur. He made a square with his fingers. His hands were brown, his nails dirty. "Our father was in the tapestry business."

"Papa wet them down," said Uncle Danny. "Shrunk them to size."

While Simon was shrinking rags up front, he was stretching laws in the basement: He fenced goods firemen liberated from burning buildings on the Lower East Side. The collection got so big that in 1914 the cops decided to take inventory. "Pots, pans, jewelry, silverware, credenzas . . ." said Uncle Danny, reading an account of the bust from a newspaper clipping he kept in his wallet. Among the confiscated merchandise were four sofas, a grand piano and a mounted Bengal tiger.

"I had to borrow money from my grandfather to bail him out of jail," raged Uncle Danny. "Borrow! From my grandfather! Had to *beg* him! The miserably spiteful bastard charged us interest! It was criminal. And all the while they tried to break Papa's mind. 'Name names,' they said. But he wouldn't sing. They could never make him sing."

"Sing that song he always sang?" said Uncle Arthur, not quite absorbing the story. "The one about the rag man?"

"The Any Rags song?"

"Yeah."

"Any rags?" Uncle Danny sang squeakily.

* * *

Any rags?
Any bags, any bones any bottles today?
It's the same old story in the same old way.

"Our father wanted Danny to be a cantor," said Uncle Arthur.

"*Mama* wanted me to be a cantor," corrected Uncle Danny. "I was just Bar Mitzvah. I was thirteen, fourteen, like that." He stretched in his chair. He had spindly white arms and a Bronx pallor. My frail, pallid uncle.

He sang a little Yiddish tune, then translated: "Like always you should be happy."

"Our grandmother had fourteen kids," volunteered Uncle Arthur.

"Ten lived," said Uncle Danny inscrutably.

"What happened to the others?" I asked.

Uncle Danny shifted his feet in the pan of water.

"Dead, dead, dead and dead. In those days, children were expendable."

My mother's dying, I thought, as I sat in the heavy shadow, listening to Uncle Danny dig up dead children from his youth. I wondered how she would die. I remembered the spooky picture she kept over her bureau. Three small children staring directly at the camera. Two boys with enormous bows under their chins and a very serious little girl with a high lace collar. They were her mother's brothers and sister. My grandmother had been the youngest of four children. The baby of the family, she got to sleep with her parents, while the other three had to share a room. One night the pilot went out in the gas lamp and they died in their sleep.

Dying must be like that, I thought. A slow, peaceful sleep with the lights out. Grown-ups died when they got old and stiff.

My mother was beginning to look old. I heard her moan at night, and it frightened me. But within my uncles' cavern of newspapers, I wasn't afraid. Nothing came in here except what Uncle Arthur dragged home from the remnants of other people's lives.

I heard Uncle Danny drone on in the shadows. He retrieved story after story from his oral annals. Simon once fastened onto the idea that he could paddle a canoe up the East River to work at Grand Central. Uncle Danny recalled the amazing sight of his father Simon carrying a canoe on his head, a voyageur on Orchard Street, the canoe riding the black waves of the teeming masses of Orthodox beards, *kepahs* and *struemmels*. Simon sucking eggs for breakfast. Simon recording all his "grievances" on cards he filed in a small wooden box. Simon set the pattern for eccentricity that his sons later elaborated into rococo.

Uncle Danny abruptly stopped. He looked at his brother. Uncle Arthur had been rummaging through a box of radio parts and cut his thumb on some jagged metal. He just sat there, with rills of blood trickling down onto a bale of papers. Uncle Danny led him gently into the bathroom, washed out the cut and smeared black salve into it. Then he wrapped a napkin around the wound and taped it. "There's only one thing that can heal a cut," Uncle Arthur said, speaking at last. He took a piece of chalk out of his pocket and wrote "T-I-M-E" on the bathroom door.

"Time for bed," said Uncle Danny. He bathed four times a day, and wanted us, to, too. "If you don't wash behind you ears," he said, "French fries will sprout."

"Great!" I thought, only pretending to wash up for bed. I changed into my pajamas and squatted over the bathroom sink, looking for the spud farm behind my ears.

Usually at bedtime my mother read to me from a big picture book of Greek and Roman legends. I loved the heroes of mythology. Theseus was my favorite. He was bold and courageous, a reckless adventurer. I liked how he had been bound in chains of forgetfulness for trying to kidnap Persephone from the Underworld.

"What should I dream about?" I'd ask my mother.

"Dream about how Theseus smote the Minotaur in the Labyrinth," she'd say.

For weeks, I'd been having a repeating nightmare. She called it my infinity dream. I stood on a checkerboard two squares from my father. "Jump," he said. I jumped toward him, but somehow landed four squares away. Every jump I took doubled the distance until we were separated by an infinity of squares. I'd wake up in a sweat.

"What should I dream about?" I asked Uncle Danny.

"Have a butter dream," he said.

"A what?"

Uncle Danny burst into a chorus of "Row, row, row your boat":

> . . . Merrily, merrily, merrily, merrily,
> Life's a butter dream.

Uncle Arthur consulted his well-used paperback about dreams. "Butter means an increase in wealth," he intoned.

Uncle Arthur collected dreams. A cardboard box at bedside cradled fifteen years' worth, all written down and alphabetized on the backs of bank deposit slips annotated with his whimsical interpretations. "If I dream about shoelaces," he said, "I file it under F, for foot. I got at least A to Y. I don't know if there's any Zs in there. I had a dream about a zebra, but I got that under animals."

"It's important to have documentation," agreed Uncle Danny.

"You know 'My father died at the age of three'?" I asked Uncle Danny.

"Sidney?" said Uncle Arthur.

"It's a poem my dad wrote about his dad."

"Sidney's dad died when he was three?"

" 'My father died at the age of three, the age applied not to him, but me.' "

"Sidney died at the age of three?"

"No, his father."

"His father was three?"

"No *my* father was. His father was older."

"So was my father."

"It's the same father."

"Mine wasn't three."

"Three what?" said Sandy drowsily.

"Papa was fifty-three," Uncle Danny said. "He died March fifteenth, nineteen twenty. The same day they assassinated Caesar."

"Caesar was assassinated in nineteen twenty?" asked Uncle Arthur.

"No," said Uncle Danny. "Papa."

My uncles had set out mattresses side by side in a newspaper nest. Sandy slept with Uncle Arthur, I got Uncle Danny. Uncle Arthur dozed off almost instantly. I could tell by the tumbling thunder of his snores. Sandy was still awake. I knew she couldn't sleep without a night light but was too timid to ask for one.

"Do you have a night light, Uncle Danny?" I said. Brave boys didn't need night lights. I was embarrassed. But it was clear Sandy would never ask, and I felt bad for her.

"Arthur does, but he's asleep. I'll ask him in the morning."

Our mattress seemed to be stuffed with crockery shards. Uncle Danny wasn't asleep either.

"Damned actors! They're sending vibrations through the floor again."

Suddenly, Uncle Danny grabbed me. I was

dumbfounded. I squirmed to get away, but the more I struggled, the tighter he held me. I knew Uncle Danny didn't mean any harm: He held me out of some avuncular instinct. I was a Lidz boy, like the rest of them.

I told myself Uncle Danny was trying to make me feel like I did when I crawled into bed with my mother after an infinity dream. Usually, she waited until I stopped crying, then sent me back to my own bed. But lately she'd been letting me stay. She held me tight, too. Very tight. Sometimes I felt her chest heave, but I didn't know what to do. I lay quiet in her arms. I fought to stay awake. I didn't want to wake up with my mother dead beside me.

Through the gloaming of my uncles' apartment, I could see Sandy was awake, too. She stared at me in Uncle Danny's death grip. Neither of us knew what to do. She began to whimper.

"It's all right," I whispered. Just saying that made me feel better.

"Are you OK?"

"I'm OK."

After what seemed forever, Uncle Danny unfolded himself from around me, got up and headed for the bathroom to take his final bath of the day. I heard his voice:

> Singing in the bathtub,
> Happy once again,
> Watching all my troubles,
> Go swimming down the drain.

Now I was crying, too, silently shielding my face in the pillow so Sandy couldn't see. Why hadn't I listened to my mother? I wished I had never come.

I stood up and slowly picked my way toward the odd shuttered door of the bathroom. Peeking through the slats, I saw Uncle Danny in the tub; he wore bathing trunks! Retreating quickly, I slapped my hand over my mouth so he wouldn't hear me as laughter replaced the tears.

Probing the walls tentatively, I tried to retrace my steps down the corridors of fusty newspapers, but in no time I was lost in this labyrinth. A teetering pillar of jars, furniture and engine parts began to slide down around me.

"UNCLE DANNNNNNY . . . !"

"HELLLLLLLLP . . . . !"

I flailed my hands at the wall of papers. Clutching the scarab in my pajama pocket, I took deep breaths, inhaling mouthfuls of dust. I heard Uncle Danny mumbling somewhere. Could he have thought I was one of the actors? Where was my sister?

"SAAAAAAAAANDY . . . . . !"

I heard something scuffle toward me through the confusion of boxes and papers. Visions of Langley Collyer crawling through his burrows with food for his brother and the huge rats that nibbled his body to bits rose up before me. I was breathing heavily—wheezing—the asthma kicking in. My throat constricted. I took long, deep breaths. I felt like I was back in the oxygen tent, only now everything was black and impenetrable.

"No one will ever find us," said the invisible king.

"Sure they will. We'll get out. You'll see."

"We're going to die here."

"Stop it! My father will save us. He's got to."

When my wheezing finally subsided, I sank down on the floor and sang another verse of Uncle Danny's bathtub song, the one he taught me for my sixth birthday, the one I sang at night to drown out the sound of my mother's moaning. The louder she moaned, the louder I sang:

> Singing to the soapsuds,
> Life is full of hope,
> You can sing with feeling,
> While feeling for the soap.

Now I too sang and rocked in the apartment, sang and rocked like Uncle Danny, back and forth, back and forth until I fell asleep. In the morning I saw him at the end of the tunnel of papers, so close I could almost have reached out and touched him during the night.

He was sitting up on the edge of his mattress speaking a strange language, a burlap bag beneath him. There was a box tied to his head, and thongs bound so tightly to his arms that the skin bulged out ghostly white.

Uncle Danny, the Orthodox Jew, the student of Hebrew, the teller of tales, the repository of family history, was saying his morning prayers, davening according to the precepts of the Torah. In the dusty morning light, the black artifacts of Jewish prayer and Uncle Danny's doleful voice came together to make me sad and lonely and fearful.

I crawled over to Uncle Danny and sat beside him while he prayed. "Amen," he said with finality, and the night was over.

"Want a hot butter sandwich?" he asked. This meant toast.

"Do you have cereal?" I asked.

"We got lots," said Uncle Arthur from the bathroom. They did. An entire wall, in fact, like a supermarket.

I looked at Sandy, who was by then out of bed and sitting quietly on a crate of dresser handles by the door. She was ready to go home. We had shared something for the first time last night: a look across the mattresses. I felt a surge of protectiveness toward her.

Uncle Danny passed us bowls of corn flakes. He handed me a half-pint of milk. It was frozen, and thunked into my bowl like an iceberg. The next thing he did was take the tea kettle and pour boiling water over the cereal. The flakes floated limply in the hot, watery liquid.

Uncle Arthur asked me what I had dreamed about.

How far could I bend the rules in a house that seemed to have none? "Tushies," I blurted out. "I had a tushie dream." It was the dirtiest word I could make myself say.

"A what?" asked Uncle Arthur.

"A tushie!"

"I'm telling Mommy what you said," threatened Sandy, our camaraderie hardly outlasting the night.

Uncle Arthur had misheard me. "A toupee," he mumbled. He thumbed through his dream book. "That means 'a death in the family.' "

"Oh no," said Sandy.

"Mama died in this apartment," said Uncle Danny.

"How?" I asked.

"It was the flu. She caught the flu, or that's what they said. I think it was vibrations. Damned actors! It was a terrible death. She shivered and shook and screamed. Oh, did she scream! We thought she was getting better, but, really, she never did. She turned yellow!"

A knock at the door. My father. We raced into his arms, quickly backtracked to kiss our uncles, and left them blinking at the door. My father hoisted us up on his hips.

"Still collecting newspapers, Arthur?" my father asked, as if realizing it for the first time.

"You collect science magazines," said Uncle Arthur.

"Mine are useful."

"So are Arthur's," said Uncle Danny. "You want to read about the atom bomb, you want to read about the Korean war, you want to read about FDR, Arthur's got the paper."

"He never looks at these papers."

"You ever read all those magazines?"

My father shook his head. As he carried us down the steps, I asked, "What's the flu?"

"Influenza," he said.

My mother was waiting in the car. "Did you have fun?" she asked.

"It was great," I said. Why did I feel I should have said, "You were right, Mommy. It wasn't so great."

"See, Selma," said my father. "I told you there was nothing to worry about."

I waited until we got on Sunrise Highway before asking, "Mommy, what's influenza?"

"A cold," she said. "A very bad cold."

Chapter 5

Ever Heard a Moth Bawl?

Snow slanted in hard over the black iron gates and drifted back in soft flurries to touch the white marble and melt on the names of the dead.

My sister crossed her arms and hugged herself tightly against the chill. My father draped his new overcoat over her shoulders. Uncle Arthur placed his rumpled one over mine. The wool scratched and smelled of mothballs and sweat. Uncle Danny was praying.

The windblown snow felt cold and wet as I watched mourners at other graves grieve over their loved ones. The snow piled thick at the base of the headstones, obscuring the debris of sorrow: notes and wreathes and flowers, many, many flowers—daisies and roses and small round yellow chrysanthemums.

The silence grew long and choked around me as Uncle Danny composed himself to begin the Mourner's Kaddish.

"Yisgadal v'yiskadash sh'may rabo . . ."

Uncle Danny seemed to expand at the gravesite.

His voice deepened. He leaned into his text, brandishing his black leather prayer book, spreading wide his arms, searching back and forth among us, stabbing with his fingers, rising up and bending down.

". . . *Yisborach v'yishtabach, v'yispoar v'yisromam* . . ."

The ancient prayer rumbled on. The wind picked up. Uncle Arthur tugged vaguely at his whiskers. Sandy started to cry.

". . . *Olaynu v'al kol yisroayl v'imru Omayn.*"

Amen.

We had buried my pet moth, Cecrops.

My father had brought the moth home from Port Jervis. He'd caught it for me outside his lab. It was a giant cecropia, a shimmering smudge of red, white and black. "The name comes from the Greek king Cecrops," my father informed me. "He was half man, half dragon." We put Cecrops in an apothecary jar with twigs and leaves, and kept him on a shelf in the garage. Each day before breakfast I wrestled open the heavy garage door so I could watch him fluttering and flurrying inside the glass.

I kept Cecrops in the garage because our new maid, Mamie, didn't want him in the house. I appeased this maid because I liked her. She baked cookies and commiserated with me about school. Mamie was the most sympathetic of the series of maids who took care of us when my mother began to spend weeks at a time in the hospital.

I had waited all week for my father to come

home from work. My mother was back from a three-week stay in the hospital. Uncle Danny and Uncle Arthur were coming for a visit in the morning and I hadn't seen them since my eighth birthday, more than a year before. I'd been keeping their presents in my bed for good luck. Uncle Danny's scarab, Uncle Arthur's Spaldeen.

Early the next morning, before my uncles arrived, I tried an experiment. I wrote my name and address on the Spaldeen and flushed it down the basement toilet, hoping it would join the other lost balls saved from the ocean by Uncle Arthur. Wouldn't he be pleased to find my name on it? But the Spaldeen swirled down the bowl, pink and rosy, and lodged in the pipes. When I flushed again, the waters rose nearly to overflowing.

I beat it out of there, retreating to the garage to take a look at Cecrops. Cold rain fell in a thin, dirty mist like a lace shawl that's been worn too long between washings. It darkened the house and glistened in the driveway and filmed on the Chevy. I opened the garage door. Cecrops was in his jar on the shelf next to the lawn mower. He clung to a twig, chilled, it seemed to me, like a dead leaf. I'd warm him in the sun, I thought. But the garage door was stuck. I gave it a yank to pull it down and the jar squirted out from between my arms, smashing on the asphalt. Picking through the shards, I tried to rescue the twitching moth. A fine gray powder dusted my sleeves. Blood dripping from a cut in the palm of my hand. I ran to the house, holding Cecrops gingerly between my fingertips.

"Is Cecrops dying, Mom?"

She drove me to the emergency room. I hardly noticed the gash or the blood or the familiar antiseptic smell that sometimes clung to my mother when she came home from one of her hospital stays.

I came home with my hand bandaged. There was no sign of Cecrops. No scattered twigs. No shattered glass. No wounded moth. My father had cleaned up.

I found him getting some tools in the basement. "Where's the moth?" I asked.

"Did the doctor give you a butterfly bandage?" said my father.

"The moth. What happened to the moth?"

"Or did he wing it?" He clamped a playful hammerlock on me. It took all of my strength to break the grip.

"Daddy, where is Cecrops?"

"What did the entymologist tell his nagging wife?"

"Daddy!"

"Don't bug me."

I ran upstairs to the kitchen and burst in on my mother. "The moth is dead," I announced. I said it matter-of-factly. "The moth is dead."

"Yes, the moth is dead," confirmed my mother.

"Cecrops is dead!" Sandy cried. Not "the moth is dead," but "Cecrops is dead." Personal, tragic. I tried to act as insouciant as my father, but I was on the verge of tears, too. "Cecrops is dead," I repeated.

"Yes, I expected it," said my mother. I winced. How could she have *expected* it to die?

"Do we have to throw him away now?" asked Sandy, sniffling.

"Not exactly. We'll bury him."

"But Daddy's already got rid of him," I said.

"Sid!" called my mother. She called several times before he sauntered into the room. "Where have you been?"

"In the basement. Dismantling the toilet. It was stopped up."

"Sid, please go get the moth. The kids want to give him a funeral."

"A what?" my father said incredulously. "A funeral? For a moth? That's ridiculous."

"Sid, stop avoiding the issue."

"What issue? Are we starting a pet cemetery? Next I'll have to get a poodle and kill it. Wouldn't that be a doggone shame. Do you think it should urn its way or . . ."

"Sid! Will you stop! Just shut up and think for a minute."

I stared. I realized my parents were arguing. Lately, my mother just seemed to tire of my father's jokes. She always wanted to be serious.

My father turned to me, peeved, embarrassed. "Don't you have homework to do?" he said.

"His hand is bandaged," my mother said.

"Well, shouldn't you be studying?"

"On Saturday morning?" I said.

"Just go outside for a while and bang a ball against the side of the house."

"It's snowing!" It was true. The rain had turned to a gray sleet.

"Why are you yelling at him, Sid?" my mother said.

"I'm not yelling!"

"Why are you so sulky?"

"I've been working on the goddamn toilet all morning!"

My mother looked at me. "Did you put anything down the toilet?"

"Don't look at *me*," I said evasively.

She looked at my father. "Sid, we're talking about the moth's funeral. The moth is dead. Honey, listen to what I'm saying. Pretty soon you're going to have to do this by yourself."

I suddenly knew they weren't just talking about the death of the moth.

My mother didn't let up. "The kids are being brought up by maids!"

"Selma, I don't have any time. I spend every spare minute reading medical journals. Where am I supposed to find the time?"

"It's not a question of time, Sid. Our children will have to depend on you."

"What's this got to do with burying some dumb moth?" said my father, clearly desperate to side-track the conversation.

"I don't know how you're going to manage the time, Sid, but you'd better!"

It was my mother who suggested he help me with my science project.

"What science project?" Science! My father must have grabbed at the opportunity to short-circuit their pain.

"Sid, don't you know your son is trying to prove the Shroud of Turin is real? A Catholic priest comes here every afternoon to help him."

My mother could wield her own needle.

"What priest?"

"Mom! No, I didn't, Dad. I . . . no . . . I'm not."

"I wouldn't be surprised if he converted to Catholicism."

My father looked distressed, then annoyed after realizing he'd been had. "Give me a break, Selma."

"Well, if he doesn't, it's not because of you, Sid."

I did have a science project. I was raising spiders in coffee cans in the garage. I fed them ketchup and iodine to see what color webs they'd weave, but I didn't want my father messing around with them. Once he took over a project, I never saw it again.

My mother hustled me off to the dining room.

"OK," my father called behind us. "I'll help him."

"Great!" I thought. His help was the last thing I wanted. I wished I *had* left earlier to do my homework. Mostly I wished they would stop arguing.

"You don't have to help me, Dad. Really."

He had already screwed up my mythology project. I loved the mythology class I took for extra

credit. I told him I wanted to make a model of Theseus smiting the Minotaur.

"I've got a better idea," he said. "Let's build Ham-
murabi's tablet." He worked in the basement for
three nights creating a plaster replica. I never laid a
finger on it.

When my report card came I had a sixty-five in
Spanish, a sixty-eight in mythology. Spanish I could
understand. But the sixty-eight in mythology? I
cried all the way home at the injustice to my father.

My mother settled me down with milk and cookies. She stroked my head. "It's all right," she said.
"It's not your fault." When I stopped sobbing, we
got in the Rambler and drove to school. The
teacher was just leaving. "There's obviously been a
mistake," said my mother.

The teacher looked over the report card and
apologized. She agreed she'd made an error. Not
the sixty-five in Spanish, but the sixty-eight in mythology. She offered an eighty-six. My mother held
out for a ninety-one.

My father was furious. "Ninety-one!" he thun-
dered. "Doesn't she know all the work I put into
that tablet?"

I didn't want the same kind of help with my spiders. I looked at my mother in total distress.

To my relief, she dropped the science project
idea, but pounced on something even worse. "OK,
Sid," she said. "I want your son to be Bar Mitzvah."

"*What?*" he said.

"What?" I said.

"You heard me, Sid. I want him Bar Mitzvah."

"But Selma, boys don't get Bar Mitzvah when they're nine."

"Of course they don't, Sid. But he has to start his classes right now."

"Mom! I don't want to go to those dumb classes. I hate Hebrew school. Besides, they've already started. They won't let me in until next year."

"I'll talk to the rabbi."

I knew from the way my father surrendered that the rabbi would, too.

Just before lunch the doorbell rang: Uncle Danny and Uncle Arthur, feathered with snow. They'd slogged the three miles from the train station.

"Why didn't you phone?" asked my father. "You know we'd have picked you up."

"We did phone!" huffed Uncle Danny.

"Collect," said Uncle Arthur.

Uncle Danny was roiling. "Dirty bastard operator! Dirty rotten bastard! Tells me to give her my name. *Orders* me! 'Never, you harlot!' Then I hung up."

The dining room table became submerged under Uncle Arthur's booty: burnt-out light bulbs, ham radio parts, watches without hands, spigots without handles, gloves without fingers, washers, nuts, bolts, the bell off a bike, wire, a spark plug, aggies, a tire guage, three Band-Aids, another Spaldeen.

"That looks like the one I just fished out of the toilet," said my father.

"It's different," I said, looking it over. "That one

had my name and address on it." I peered at my mother guiltily.

"Didn't you just tell me you hadn't put anything down the toilet?" she asked sharply.

"No."

"Then what *did* you say?"

"I said, 'Don't look at me.' "

My mother sighed. "You're more like your father every day."

"What's wrong with your hand?" asked Uncle Arthur.

"Cecrops is dead," I said.

"Who's Cecrops?"

"The first king of Athens," said my father.

"What did they do to him?" demanded Uncle Danny.

"He got smashed. There was glass all over the driveway. I cut my hand. Now he's dead."

"Who's Cecrops?"

"The inventor of writing."

"Those spiteful bastards!"

"He was alive when I left, but when I came back from the hospital, Daddy had thrown him in the trash."

"Who's Cecrops?"

"The go-between of Athena and Poseidon."

"Sidney's a pimp?"

"My moth."

"Cecrops. That's a funny name. It doesn't rhyme with moth at all."

"He introduced the bloodless sacrifice, the burial of the dead . . ."

"Funny they should get you to dispose of the corpse, Sidney."

My father stirred from his relentless pedagogic non-sequiturs. "What the hell are you talking about now, Danny?"

"The murder. The evidence. The coverup."

"I didn't kill that moth. It was already dead."

"Oh, now you change the story."

"I'm not changing anything! We're talking about a goddamn moth!"

"Don't make it any worse."

My mother began clearing Uncle Arthur's junk off the dining room table. She dropped most of it in the trash. Uncle Arthur didn't even notice.

"Mommy said we can bury Cecrops," I said.

"It's absurd to bury pets," grumbled my father.

"What about people, Sid?" asked my mother.

"You gave your cat one, Sid," said Uncle Arthur.

"Gave my cat what?"

"A funeral. Remember? You buried her at Grant's Tomb."

"That was different. That was so when people asked, 'Who's buried at Grant's Tomb,' I could say, 'My cat.'"

"I wanna bury my moth *here*," I wailed.

"Where did they bury President Grant then?" Uncle Arthur asked.

"In the tomb," exclaimed my father. "The tomb! The tomb! The tomb!"

"With your cat?"

"Don't be catatonic."

"I'm allergic to cats," I said.

"Great!" my father said. "I'll remember not to bury you with one."

It was fun to tangle him up in his own twisting words. But he was never shackled for long.

"Let's flush the moth down the toilet," he suggested. "We'll have a burial at sea."

"Better take it to a cemetery," said Uncle Danny. "They won't follow us in there."

"You can bury Cecrops near the flag at the cemetery in Elmont," my mother said. "It's red and white and blue, sort of like the moth. It's very pleasant to be in a cemetery. It's well kept and in the summer there are trees and flowers."

"All of that's true," allowed my father. "The problem with cemeteries is that you have to stay too long."

"Papa kept moths in his shop," said Uncle Danny. "Lived in the basement. Ate the woolens. Once I came downstairs to his workshop and saw him stooped over a candle, waving a dollar at a couple of them, batting them around. Like kittens. Some were his pets."

"What did he name them?" I asked.

"Anna, Lilly, Rose, Jennie. After his sister-in-laws, who despised him."

My father muttered something I couldn't make out.

"I'll get a box," I said, and dashed to the kitchen.

"Get something to dig with," said my mother.

I got the spatula my father used to make pancakes. I dumped Sandy's new party shoes from their box for a coffin. She didn't mind contributing to the pageantry.

My father brought in the moth on a dustpan. He sifted out the dirt, dropped the moth into the box and replaced the lid. "That's not the real moth," Uncle Danny said.

"Of course it is!"

"I don't believe you, Sidney."

"Calm yourself, Danny. Just calm yourself."

My father drove us through the snow to the outskirts of Green Acres and parked outside the cemetery's iron gates. My mother had stayed home baking cookies for the postfuneral feast. I walked along the path with Uncle Arthur, who avoided bad luck by never stepping on the cracks in the concrete.

We made our way past family plots that lined the path like little marble farms for the dead. The names on the tombstones registered like the roll my teacher read every morning: Cohen, Greenberg, Moskowitz, Weinstein. Swallowing a giggle, I looked for Lidz. When it was my turn would I have to raise my hand and say, "Here"?

The flag was in a circle of plain white gravestones with the names of soldiers on them. Uncle Danny leaned against it while paging through the prayer book he carried everywhere. Sandy and Uncle Arthur peered at names. I started to dig a hole with the spatula. The ground was muddy under the snow. My father watched impatiently, grabbed the spatula and finished the job himself.

"Boy, that hole is deep," said Uncle Arthur. We put in Sandy's shoe box and covered it with mud and Uncle Danny began his solemn and comforting Kaddish. We stood in the snow and listened to the old mournful rhythms that conduct the dead into their graves.

"Amen," he said at last.

"No moth has ever received a finer funeral," my father announced. He turned to leave, but Uncle Danny insisted on exploring the graveyard. We trailed along behind: Sandy, me, my father and Uncle Arthur. Uncle Danny found a brownstone mortuary chapel that rose from a hill. "Lantern on lantern on lantern," he said, describing the architecture. "Octagonal as in Charlemagne's chapel at Aix-la-Chappelle." His fund of esoteric knowledge easily matched my father's.

We passed elegant and dignified slate tombstones, round-shouldered as Uncle Arthur; an obelisk, graven with designs like the ones on Uncle Danny's prayer book, and a marble fountain gleaming with pennies and nickels. Uncle Arthur sat on its edge, alternately splashing his hand in the icy water and shoving it into his pocket.

Uncle Danny continued to the eastern wall of the cemetery. We stopped at the grave of a little boy.

"I'll never forgive them for Max," said Uncle Danny. "I will not. I must not."

"My mother's youngest brother," Uncle Arthur said, trotting up from the fountain. "Danny and him were good friends. Until he got run over by a truck."

"They wouldn't tell me until after the funeral," Uncle Danny said. " 'He's dead, gone,' they said. 'That's all you need to know,' they said. I didn't believe them. I wanted to see for myself. They wouldn't let me. I went to the cemetery anyway. But there was only dirt. New dirt shoveled on old dirt."

"I think I found Cecrops!" said Sandy, peering at a tombstone.

My father took a look. "It's a dead leaf," he said judiciously.

"But it's a pretty dead leaf," said Uncle Arthur.

"What are tombstones for?" I asked.

"Identification," said my father.

"Don't be foolish, Sidney," said Uncle Danny. "They're to keep the body down so it doesn't rise up and come home."

"What do you want your tombstone to say, Uncle Danny?" I said.

"Danny's epitaph," interrupted my father, "will read: What the hell are *you* looking at?"

"I don't want it to say anything," Uncle Danny said firmly. "What they don't know can't hurt me."

"Why do live people bring dead people flowers?" Uncle Danny began, "Because . . ."

". . . bodies stink," interjected my father. A plain-spoken guide, he was.

Big, wet snowflakes fell out of a dreary sky that closed in on us like a tight, gray dome.

"Where's heaven?" asked Sandy.

"In the minds of morons," snapped my father.

"Mommy says that's where Cecrops went."

"A moth's life cycle is continually evolving: infinite, without beginning or end. The cycle itself is diplontic because the body cells of an adult moth contain two identical . . ."

"You're wrong, Sidney," said Uncle Danny.

"What?"

"When you desert the beliefs of your fathers, you're in Gehenna, Sidney. It happens. One day."

"Bullshit!"

"You must cling to the old rituals or they'll take control."

"Religion is a crutch, Danny. And only cripples need crutches."

"A crutch is not bad, Sidney. A crutch gives cripples support. And all of us are cripples in some way, even FDR. And he became president."

"Was President Grant a cripple, too?" asked Uncle Arthur.

My father flung up his hands and headed for the car. "Arthur," said Uncle Danny. "Give the children money to mark the moth's grave."

Uncle Arthur was eying the coin fountain. He reached into his pocket and pulled out a handful of pennies.

"Uncle Arthur," said Sandy. "Your pennies are wet."

Uncle Arthur blushed and dried them on his sleeve.

On the way back we stopped for hot chocolate at a diner that advertised: ALL YOU CAN DRINK, 20 CENTS. My father relaxed. "Get me turtle soup," he told the guy at the grill, "and make it snappy."

"That's the first time I heard that one," the counterman said. "Today."

We finished our hot chocolate. My father asked for seconds. "That will be another twenty cents each," said the counterman.

"But the sign says 'All You Can Drink,'" argued my father.

"Sure it does. It means that's all you *can* drink for twenty cents."

"Nobody in their right mind would read it that way."

"I did," said Uncle Danny.

"That just proves my point."

"You don't know, Sidney, you don't know. For once can't you just admit you misread a simple sign?"

"Shut up, Danny," snarled my father. "Shut up. Shut *up!*"

My father simmered and stewed. When we got up to leave, he put a quarter inside a glass of water, covered it with a place mat, turned it over on the counter and pulled the placemat out. "A watery tip," my father said, still sore about the hot chocolate.

At home, Uncle Danny said to my mother, "Make sure Sidney doesn't go back and dig up Cecrops."

"Daddy, are you going to dig up Cecrops?" I asked.

"He wouldn't do that," said my mother. "Would you, Sid?"

My father gazed out the window.

"*Would* you, Sid?" my mother insisted.

"No, but it's not a bad idea."

"Sidney Lidz!"

I don't think my father meant to be mean, but he could only compromise so much. It was as if he already knew that he wouldn't be able to fill the vacuum of my mother's absence, and so instead he could only accelerate the spin of chaos.

"This whole afternoon has been asinine," he said. "First, shit rises from the toilet. Then I take shit for not working on a science project I never heard of. Then I've got to listen to shit about moths going to heaven. Jesus Christ, moths in heaven! Everything I stand for is to have these kids not believe in heaven, and you tell them dead moths end up there. I shouldn't have even bothered coming home. Next time, I'll take a rocket to Venus."

"You should pack a good lunch, Sidney," said Uncle Danny.

"He's right," seconded Uncle Arthur. "You might not like what they have to eat there."

My father was fuming when he left the kitchen. "Look," I told Sandy. "He's going into the garage." We watched. "He's going to get something to dig up Cecrops. He's . . ." My mother stared at me taunting Sandy, but said nothing. She seemed fragile and fatigued. I saw disappointment in her face. The moth's funeral had not provided the solace she wanted to bring us. Her family was crumbling into discord.

"Can we go back some day to see the moth's grave?" Sandy asked my father when he returned.

"We'll see," he said. We never did.

The next time we went to a cemetery, we buried my mother.

Chapter 6

Venus Envy

The fine mist of the vaporizer diffused light and sound. I felt as if I were in a hissing fog. It was the morning of the fifth-grade science fair and I was in bed getting over an asthma attack. Overhead the light fixture loomed like God's eye, and around it clicked and clacked a spinning universe of model rockets and satellites and planets my father had created to take my mind off my asthma. Colored balls bobbled in fishing tackle and coat-hanger wire orbits, curious spokes and webs in which I saw the complex rings of Saturn, sunbaked Mercury, Mars pocked with craters. The sixty-watt sun glared white off the cotton clouds of Venus; the planet streaked across the ceiling like a sudden memory. It was the closest planet to Earth, yet in my father's arrangement, Venus looked the farthest away. His ordered solar system circled over me morning and night. I knew it was there even when the sun was turned out.

"Anybody home?" he called from the hall. "It's time to go!"

I pretended I was darting through the Venusian drizzle on a reconnaissance mission.

"We'd better turn back," said the invisible king. "Your father's not here."

"He's here," I said. "We'll find him."

My father was rounding up my sister and me to visit my mother at the hospital on the way to the science fair. He seemed more distracted than ever.

"So what have you been up to this morning?" he asked, not noticing the invisible king. Sandy wandered in behind him.

"Flying around Venus."

"Fine," he said, unhearing. He turned to Sandy and said with equal remoteness, "And what about you?"

I got up and got dressed and we left to go off to see my mother, the three of us disconnected into our own universes.

Actually, Venus had become my father's latest preoccupation. *Mariner,* the first interplanetary space probe, was about to be launched. He felt it justified his faith in technology. *Mariner* was taking a payload of scientific instruments: cameras and remote sensors ready for the first close-up examination of Venus. My father loved the idea of all that data spewing across millions of miles to Earth.

"Who cares about pictures of Venus?" I'd once ventured. "All we'll see is some dumb planet."

"All we'll see!" my father bristled. "What could be more fantastic than another world?" My father looked to the universe for what Uncle Arthur searched for in gutters and Uncle Danny suspected in the faces of passersby.

The night before my father had set up his telescope in the backyard of our new house in the Philadelphia suburbs. He scanned the heavens reciting passages from Spinoza.

"Who's Spinoza?" I asked.

"The seventeenth-century Dutch metaphysician," he replied.

"What's a metaphysician?"

"I never metaphysician who didn't overcharge."

He was always setting me up. But he couldn't resist adding a straight answer. He told me with relish that Spinoza had been expelled from his synagogue for unorthodoxy and that he had to patch together a living as a lens grinder. Under the waning moon my father read to me from the *Ethics:* "Truth is the criterion of itself and of the false," he said, "as light manifests itself and the dark." The words were strange and incomprehensible, but exhilarating, too. They've become forever wedded to my father's voice and the memory of looking through a telescope on a starry night.

We'd moved to Philadelphia during a snowstorm in 1961. My father didn't like the place any better than he did Long Island, but we needed the money. My mother's medical bills seemed infinite and a hi-fi company offered him a higher salary to run its engineering department. So we settled into a ranch house that sat on a small hill at a crazy angle, shaded by a windbreak of evergreens and hidden from the road by a sweet gum tree. The tree so obscured the view from the street that no matter where you stood, you could never see the whole house. My father pruned diligently, but never enough to allow the house to be wholly revealed to the neighbors.

The suburbs of Philadelphia were as unknown to him as the surface of Venus, and a lot less intriguing. He had a New Yorker's distaste for Philadelphia's provincialism, its pretensions, its massive inferiority complex. I remember him dismissing a flyer for something called the Philadelphia Cultural Society. "Philadelphia culture is an oxymoron," he sniggered. "Like Midwestern charm."

He retreated from Philadelphia culture into his basement workshop. The shelves were crowded with crates of silver screws and bolts and washers; wide gray clusters of resistors, transistors, and transformers; green and gold knobs in an amazing variety of shapes and sizes; tawny ratchets and rusty wrenches; cathode ray tubes, sonar detectors, Geiger counters, power drills, lawn mowers—the Tinkertoys of modern technology. Everywhere was the exquisite odor of molten solder. This was the site on which my science project was constructed. Originally, I had wanted to make a scale model of the Berlin Wall out of Frosted Flakes. "That's silly," he said. He had grander ideas for me. "The Venus Probe," he said. "We'll build our own *Mariner*."

Nested within piles of journals and blueprints and research materials, ensconced behind his black drafting table, his black glasses and his black two-day stubble, my father looked like a benign Mephistopheles at work on his memoirs. But he was demonic only in the energy he devoted to our *Mariner*. He fitted it with enough electronic ganglia to have jump-started Frankenstein's monster.

At first I watched keenly, but later I would merely check in once or twice a day. I began to hate my science project—it had slipped away from me like all my other projects and become my father's.

"You're contributing as much as me," he said.

"How?"

"Well, you're writing all the captions."

Which was true. On a scroll of plastic sheeting I was charting *Mariner*'s intended trajectory and recording all the facts my father rammed into me: "The nineteen-inch microwave radiometer makes one hundred and twenty-degree scanning motions at wavelengths of thirteen point five and nineteen millimeters; the nine thousand eight hundred solar panels weigh forty-eight pounds each and generate up to two hundred and twenty watts of power; the spacecraft needs to travel more than one hundred and eighty million miles in one hundred and nine days to traverse the twenty-six-million-mile distance at inferior conjunction." I wrote it down, but it was about as clear to me as Spinoza.

My father reassured me. "Everything can be broken down into numbers," he said. "That's why science—pure science—will be Earth's ultimate salvation."

Science wasn't saving my mother. Her hospital stays were becoming longer and longer; I measured them by the nights that she was away. And I didn't like it now when she was home. She had become unpredictable. She wasn't dying like some movie heroine. She could be sullen and bad-tempered. I resented her.

I saw her weep for the first time when I was ten. She had been home from the hospital for about a week when the doctor came to see her. I was in my bedroom across the hall pretending to be doing my homework.

"I'm going to have to put you back in the hospital, Selma," the doctor said.

"I'm not going back," my mother cried. "I'm not going back."

But she went back. On the morning of the science fair, my father was tense and anxious. He was in such a rush that Sandy and I didn't even have breakfast. He bought us candy bars at a gas station. He argued with the traffic all the way to the hospital. "Don't they time the lights? That's my lane, you idiot! Are you blind? Yield, the sign says, asshole! Can't anyone drive in this goddamn city?"

Uncle Danny and Uncle Arthur had heard about the science fair and decided to come down from the Bronx for the day.

"Meet us at the hospital," my father had told Uncle Arthur.

"Leo's or Harry's?" came the reply.

"Selma's!" Uncle Leo was at Rockland State Hospital an hour west of New York City, soothing his demons with arts and crafts. Uncle Harry was up around Buffalo at Gowanda State Hospital, recounting his boxing victories.

My father told Uncle Arthur we'd visit my mother, then drop Sandy off at the home of one of her friends.

We found Uncle Danny perched on a car in the parking lot, waving his prayer book and blasting away at a couple of nurses, his face red with righteous anger. In one hand he held a book of matches, in the other, an unlit match. "Phonies!" Uncle Danny raged at the women in their starched white uniforms. "You're all cardboard and cellophane. I see right through you! Poisonous, squirming worms! Get near me and I'll incinerate you."

"What the hell are you doing, Danny?" my father said. "This is a hospital." He grabbed him by the lapel and dragged him across the asphalt driveway into the waiting room. We followed.

My father found us a corner away from the elevators, away from the nurses' station, away from anyone who might be spooked by these moonstruck men.

"Cellophane citizens!" Uncle Danny groused. "Strictly Saran Wrap, Sidney. Ever met anyone who wasn't transparent?"

"Yes."

"Neither have I."

I sank into a plump armchair covered with shabby gold damask. Across from me, my uncles sat side by side on a battered wooden bench. My father went off with Sandy to get my mother, who liked to have time to make herself up for visitors—even when they were only her fruitcakey brother-in-laws.

Uncle Arthur was his old self. He had towed in a small sack of mementos culled from the junk in his apartment. He fished out a nine-volt battery, a model-train transformer, his new hearing aid. Watching helped me pass the time as I waited.

With special care, Uncle Arthur wound up the clothesline that had bound the sack.

"Once Papa hung from this clothesline by his teeth," Uncle Danny said. Simon had performed his high wire act outside the Lidz Button Company, where he worked for his cousins, Sol, Isaiah and Israel. He'd fitted the back of his teeth with a mouthpiece. "By his teeth Papa hung over Orchard Street with his cousins hanging onto *him*."

Uncle Danny pulled forth a blurred photo for proof. All I could see was three dots hanging from a fourth.

"Look how high," urged Uncle Arthur.

"One hundred and twenty feet up," said Uncle Danny. "Papa had strong teeth."

I marveled. I wondered how they got down. I wondered how they got up. My grandfather the fence was a Superman.

I looked around for my father. He seemed to have been away a long time.

From his sack, Uncle Arthur withdrew a banged-up cheese-box filled with file cards. And Uncle Danny told another story. "Papa's grievances," he explained. Uncle Arthur withdrew, Uncle Danny explained.

Uncle Danny gave me the card labeled PETS. I read Simon's complaint about the unfriendly dog that lived in the next apartment.

CHECKER PLAYERS had one entry: Richard Jordan, checkers champ. Uncle Danny told me that Simon had played Jordan to a draw in 1900. "A filthy cheat, Jordan was," said Uncle Danny. "Spiteful. Kicked Papa under the table. Blew smoke in his face. Wanted him to jump. But Papa wouldn't jump. Ha. Ha. Only his cousin Isaiah jumped. When the stock market crashed. Out the window."

On a card that read BUTTON MEN my grandfather had neatly written the names of Sol and Israel, two forgotten men without imagination who had rejected his idea to manufacture droopless socks you could button to your pants.

My father reappeared with Sandy. "Your mother will be here in a few minutes," he told me. "She's getting more tests."

Uncle Danny was still engrossed in Simon's grievances. "When Papa came to America, the patent office was about to shut down. They figured everything had been invented already."

"That's ridiculous, Dan," my father couldn't resist saying.

"Spinoza prophesied it."

"He did no such thing."

"Spinoza was a genius," Uncle Danny said serenely. "Sidney, a genius you're not."

"OK, a genius I'm not, but an inventor I am. I already hold seven patents. The patent office is busier than ever."

"Papa knew better than the patent office. He invented a machine that made tiny latkes, packaged them for mailing. A Latke of the Week Club, he thought of. Sent out a different latke every week. But nobody signed up. He invented a universal alphabet, so simple even Sidney could understand it."

My mother appeared at the door on a nurse's arm. Uncle Danny fell silent. She stepped into the room with a kind of fragile, regal beauty. She was wearing the pink nightgown Sandy and I had given her for Mother's Day, and the washed-out fluorescent hospital light glinted mahogany red in her hair. The bones of her face were more delicate than ever, but she swept into the plain, low-ceilinged room with the old confidence. She bunched her shoulders around Sandy and me and kissed us. We walked her back to her room and my father helped her into bed and cranked it up so she sat fully erect. A nurse brought in a tray of food.

The room was a vault of dead air. My mother shared it with a Mrs. Berman, an old woman, paralyzed and enormously fat.

Every few hours two orderlies would prop Mrs. Berman on her side and change her bedding. They always positioned her so that she wouldn't have to move her eyes from the night stand at the foot of her bed, where a clock ticked and ticked and ticked. *"Zeger!"* she yelled if someone moved one. *"Zeger! Zeger! Zeger!"*

"What does she want?" Sandy asked.

"She wants to see her clock," my mother said. *"Zeger* is Yiddish for clock."

I asked my mother if I could get her anything. "Could you bring me that soda?" she said, pointing to the console by her bed. I held the straw to her lips, which were cracked and dry but lipsticked a bright pink. She rested now, her legs drawn up thin and bare and white, her face smiling. She was pleased to hold my hand, her grip surprisingly firm.

"How's school?" she asked Sandy.

"I can't see the blackboard," Sandy said.

"Maybe she needs glasses, Sid."

"Nobody actually *sees* the blackboard," said my father. With a kind of detached tenderness, he began sponging her arms. "It's just an action of light waves on the retina."

My mother waved him to silence. "I'll make an appointment with an optometrist."

Despite her illness, she was still orchestrating her family. She paid the bills, she had conferences with my teachers over the phone, she even signed me up in an electronics course at the Franklin Institute. "It will be fun," she assured me. "You'll have something to talk to your father about."

I went to the first class, didn't understand a thing, and never went back. Instead, I'd rendezvous with my new friend, Ash, and go to the movies downtown.

She asked my father if he'd fed us breakfast.

"They've eaten," he replied.

"But have they had breakfast?" She was too weary now for his evasive word games.

"Sure we did," I said. "Daddy made us eggs before we left." I lied, feeling a kind of obligation to keep her from worrying about my father's ineptitude, and to defend him from her impatience.

"So how's the electronics course?" she asked.

"OK."

"You haven't been seeing that new boy, have you?"

"Ash?"

"Yes."

"No," I said.

"Good. He's trouble, nothing but trouble."

Ash was the neighborhood bad boy. He was a skinny kid, thin-lipped and stone-eyed. I met him at a bowling alley: He had sabotaged a spare I'd been working on by pressing the reset button just as I released the ball.

My mother didn't like Ash because she heard he had taken a neighborhood girl into the woods and bombarded her with firecrackers until she ran out of range. He liked knives, guns and things that blew up. The globe on his desk hid a small arsenal of cherry bombs and M-80s. I impressed him with the .22 my father allowed me to shoot in the basement.

His own father, a real estate tycoon in California, had shot himself when Ash was six. I overheard one of my mother's friends telling her how Ash had gotten up early one summer morning, walked downstairs to the living room of his Palo Alto home and found his dad crumpled in an easy chair. Ash never talked about it.

I was his only friend. But I was never sure if he really liked me, and at the time I didn't understand why I was drawn to him. He was genuinely strange and cruel. On Halloween he had taken apart my sister's dolls and strung the arms and legs from our gum tree, then sat back in the hedges to laugh when she found them.

"What did you do that for?" I asked Ash after Sandy ran sobbing from the house.

"You wanted me to string up Sandy?"

Ash didn't let people get close to him. He disliked being touched, even by his mother. He flinched if you brushed against his arm. He once decked a kid for accidentally messing up his hair.

He wasn't even nice to people who treated him decently. He broke every rule, but he couldn't be punished because he didn't care. Thinking back, I suppose he acted out all the dark, creepy urges I couldn't admit I even had. As hurtful as I sometimes seemed to myself, he was always worse than

I could imagine myself being. He was a rat, but I needed him to work my way through bad times.

Uncle Arthur roused himself from a deep torpor. "So Selma," he said. "They make you wear a truss?"

"What in the world for?"

"Sidney wore one before he had *his* operation."

"But he had a hernia!"

Uncle Arthur subsided back into his inertia. My mother turned to Uncle Danny, who was turned out in a lean gray suit and a red polka-dot tie. "Mind if I smoke, Danny?" she asked.

"I don't care if you *burn!*"

Sandy asked Uncle Arthur if he would go to the hospital cafeteria with her.

"I only got a buck," he said.

"You came here all the way from the Bronx and all you brought was a dollar?" exclaimed my mother.

"I figured I might need extra money for a bus."

"I'll buy lunch, Selma," my father said. "What's good here?"

"Potato salad. Potato salad, coleslaw and tuna fish."

"That's fine."

"No, it's not fine," Uncle Danny said. "You've let her manipulate us, Sidney."

"What?"

"She's decided everything. She didn't let us choose a damn thing."

"She's being helpful, Danny. She's doing us a favor."

"A favor! Do you think I don't realize she's trying to control our lives!"

"You're right, Danny," my mother said, finally losing her cool. "I want to manipulate you. I want to control you. In fact, right now I want you to *get the hell out of my room!*"

"You'll never make *me* eat that potato salad."

"Out! Get out!"

Uncle Danny steamed out of the room. "Sidney," he said, "I'll be waiting by the elevator."

"Honestly, Sid," said my mother. "Does he always have to make such a big fuss?"

"Listen, Selma," Uncle Arthur said, perking up. "Back in the apartment I've got plenty of trusses."

"I said fuss, not truss."

"Arthur," said my father. "You've got to start using your hearing aid."

"What?"

"Your hearing aid! Why don't you put it on?"

"I can't. I'll wear out the batteries."

"Sid, please!" pleaded my mother.

"Arthur, let me take you to the elevator."

Uncle Arthur brushed Mrs. Berman's clock askew on the way out.

"Zeger! Zeger!" she moaned.

I looked at her, fat and pitiful and immobile. "She's groaning," I said.

"She's all right," said my mother.

"Are you sure she's groaning?" asked Sandy.

"Listen to her," I said. "She's been doing it all morning."

I righted her clock so that she could see it again.
My mother smiled.

"You'd better leave now if you want to get to the
science fair."

With a great exertion of will, she got out of bed
and walked us to the elevator, where my uncles
waited quietly with my father. I kissed her, then
watched her lurch back to the room where Mrs.
Berman lay staring at the passage of time.

Tinkertoy technology had transformed the school
gym into a world of Plexiglas pyramids, Petri dishes
and papier-mâché missiles. We came to the Venus
Probe.

"Where'd you find that?" asked Uncle Arthur.

"I didn't find it," said my father. "I made it."

"Out of stuff I brought you?"

"Out of stuff you brought me."

Uncle Arthur grinned broadly.

Next to me, Benji Kessle had set up his particle-
beam ray gun. I hated him. He was a scientist kid,
the kind my father liked to talk to. He had watery
blue eyes that made him look as if he had stayed up
late reading *The World Book Encyclopedia*. "Particle
beams can't be aimed with any accuracy," my father
told Benji. "They'd be curved by the earth's constantly changing geomagnetic field."

"What about neutral particle beams?" asked
Benji.

"The problem is density. The beam would be so
wide at its origin that electrons would scatter be-

fore they converted to gamma rays. The only possible application I see is a neutral hydrogen beam that turns to protons the instant . . ."

I pulled him away to see the other exhibits: sprouting seeds, creaking robots, bubbling test tubes. Ash's project was labeled "The Legend of Sleepy Hologram."

"What's a hologram?" I asked my father.

"A three-dimensional image made by two beams of coherent light in the form of an interference pattern . . ."

Ash's definition of hologram was more succinct.

"Impure science," he said.

I squinted through the peephole in a grocery bag and saw his "hologram," an amazingly realistic Dixie cup. In fact, it was a Dixie cup. Uncle Danny peered in after me.

"That ham ain't kosher," he said.

"It's impure science," Ash repeated. His sneer invited alteration with a brick.

My father looked in and smirked. "Very funny. Very, very funny."

"What do you mean, sir?"

"Come on. We all get the joke."

"What joke?"

"You can't be serious."

"Serious? Of course I'm serious."

Ash, of course, was never serious. He'd caught my father, though, and I loved it.

Uncle Arthur stood by a model of the female reproductive system that warned: SIZE OF EGGS GREATLY EXAGGERATED.

"Look over there," Ash told him. "Somebody's waving to you." Uncle Arthur could barely see the greatly exaggerated eggs, even with his bifocals. He waved vaguely at the figure across the room, then started walking toward it. When Uncle Arthur finally figured out it was a life-sized cutout of an android, Ash hooted and expected me to join in. I did, but I felt like I'd turned Uncle Arthur over to the Gestapo.

Uncle Arthur wandered back unfazed. "What'd I tell you," said Uncle Danny. "Everyone here's cardboard."

Ash appraised my uncles coolly. His eyes were sunken and hooded—the left slightly more closed than the right—so he looked like he was taking continual aim at them. Ash knew about Uncle Danny. I had told him how he thought Mickey Mantle was trying to kill him. I had told him how he brandished his prayer book and threatened to set cellophane nurses on fire.

"Let's play a little joke," Ash said. He wrote out the lyrics to "Santa Claus Is Coming to Town" and XXXed out key words: "You better not XXX. You better not XXXX. You better not XXXXX, I'm telling you why. XXXXX XXXXX is coming to town. He knows when you are sleeping. He knows when you're awake. He knows when you've been XXX or XXXX."

Ash shoved the message at me. "Stick it in your uncle's prayer book," he said.

Uncle Danny stood transfixed before an experiment that showed a bowl of languid guppies in a solution of sodium amytal. It was yet another proof that his fears were justified: life forms immersed in a mind-altering drug. Ash slipped the prayer book out of Uncle Danny's coat pocket and handed it to me. I sneaked the note in somewhere between the blessings for wine and bread, and dropped the prayer book behind Uncle Danny on the floor.

"Uncle Danny," I said. "You dropped something." We stood back ready to snicker.

Uncle Danny's pale, bony hands felt the folded paper. He read the message. "Demons!" he said, his voice creaking like dry leather. I saw old pain pinch his gray face.

"What's wrong, Uncle Danny?" I asked guiltily. But he walked away without answering.

I felt I ought to go somewhere and wash my hands.

The winners were being announced, in reverse order. Barbara Gold took third place. Benji Kessle, second. "And first prize . . ." I'd won! Ash slapped me hard on the back. A little too hard.

"I'll bet you didn't make that yourself," said Benji.

"Well, my father helped me a little."

"A lot!"

"A little!"

"Creep!"

"Ratfink!"

"Cretin!"

"Oxymoron!"

I clotheslined him and soon we were rolling on the parquet floor. Mr. Sala, the health teacher, broke it up. My father, perhaps remembering my mother's advice, said: "You guys be friends. Benji, why don't you come over to our house tonight for dinner?"

"Dad!"

"It'll be fun."

"It'll be awful."

"Your mother would like it."

"Well . . . OK."

Suddenly, there was a commotion in another corner of the gym. Mr. Sala had put his hand on Ash's shoulder and Ash reacted as if he'd been violated. "Sodomist!" he screamed. "Look in the garbage cans! They're full of dead chickens with bloody assholes and smiles on their faces!"

All over the gym, jaws swung open in shocked disbelief. Mr. Sala did some earnest huffing: "Young man, I have half a mind—"

"—That's no excuse," Ash cut in, then stomped out.

Uncle Danny was outside, too, reading and re-reading the note. He looked grim and ghostly. I ran over and stood beside him. He watched me warily. I took his free hand and shook it. "I won the science fair, Uncle Danny. I won!"

Uncle Danny gave me that same blank, gray look. "I want to leave," he said tonelessly.

Uncle Arthur seemed more puzzled than usual. "Danny," he said. "You feel OK?"

"I feel OK."

"Did anything happen?"

"It happened."

"What happened?"

"Happened."

We all piled into the car: my father, my uncles, Benji, Ash and me. Uncle Danny sat up front, his tongue wagging as if he'd been charged again with an electric wire.

"What's he, a dog?" Ash cracked.

We dropped my uncles at the train station. Uncle Danny headed straight in without turning around or waving. He didn't stop until he reached Bellevue. My mother told me on my next visit that he'd committed himself that night.

It took Uncle Danny more than a year to sort out his paranoia at Bellevue. Meanwhile, Uncle Arthur tramped through the Bronx streets, enhancing his shoelace collection.

At home, my father announced plans to build a nuclear reactor out of a Bunsen burner. He and Benji went down to the basement to start. Ash and I stayed upstairs. I showed him the maze game my father had brought home from his office: a movable platform with fifty holes in it. You had to maneuver a steel ball around the holes without letting it fall through. I'd never done it, but Ash got a perfect score every time, working the controls with his toes.

When Ash got bored with the maze, we went out to the front lawn and set off some firecrackers he had in his pockets. He never left his house without a small supply of explosives. I watched his fire-crackers snap and pop and sizzle, filling the air with smoke and an acrid gunpowder smell. Ash took out his penknife and carved his initials into our sweet gum tree. My father motioned to me from the front door. "Is that the kid your mother doesn't like?"

I didn't say anything.

"I hope it's not. You know that would make her really mad." He glared at Ash and cleared his throat as if he was about to scold him. Unable to, he went back down to the basement.

"I think my mother might be dying," I said. I had never even told anyone she was sick before this moment.

"Yeah," he said, cutting his initials deeper. "I heard she's about to croak."

I felt strangely relieved. Ash's nasty bluntness made death seem sort of cool.

"That means you'll get a dog," he said.

"What?"

"They always give kids dogs when their parents croak."

"What?"

"When my father croaked, I got a cocker spaniel. Except that I didn't want a dog, so my mother took it back and got a cat."

I nodded.

"You've only got one thing to worry about."

"Huh?"

"Who's gonna make your lunch every day?"

* * *

On the day of the *Mariner* launch, my father shook me awake at three in the morning. "Come on. Get up," he said. "The Venus probe is about to take off." We went to the kitchen and listened on short-wave.

"T minus two minutes. Mark. . . . Missile power? . . . Go. . . . Propulsion? . . . Go. . . . *Mariner?* . . . Go. . . ."

It was just as my father had said it would be.

"Mission is green. . . . All systems are go! . . . Nineteen, engines stand by. . . . Ignition . . . five . . . four . . . three . . . two . . . one . . . mainstage!"

We could hear the rumble as the thrust began to build. The roar grew louder and louder, then stopped.

"Something . . . something . . . something . . . the launch . . . something . . ." The voice on the radio was becoming incoherent. "Abort! Abort! Abort!"

Someone had forgotten to feed a hyphen into the coding, and the rocket veered off course. Five minutes after liftoff the destruct button was pushed. The voice described the Venus Probe vaporizing in a brilliant flash of flame.

I looked at my father. He had a weak smile pasted on his face. He said nothing.

Chapter 7

"Crazy-Town"

Uncle Leo was a family legend, a figure more mythic than real. He impressed people. He was a father figure to my father, who was in awe of his older brother's brains until they turned peculiar. He was also awed by Uncle Leo's penis, which was a little peculiar, too. Uncle Leo's had two holes. *I* was awed when my father told me how he and Uncle Leo would get into pissing contests. They'd lock arms and write their names in the snow—Uncle Leo showing off his more elaborate double script. It was a story I could never quite get out of my head, especially when I'd go into a men's room. I always wondered whether Uncle Leo used two urinals at once, or finished in half the time it took me.

Besides being a unique calligrapher, Uncle Leo was a belles lettrist of great erudition, a Joycean of Ulyssean fussiness and a mental patient of Poundian duration. He wrote and wrote and wrote; poems, plays, novels, short stories. The Collected Uncle Leo would probably fill Uncle Arthur's back room. Reserved and intensely focused, Uncle Leo hung out like a dangling participle in the run-on sentence of his own life.

Uncle Leo found fixed purposes repugnant to his temperament and false to life. He wrote a series of essays at City College on indeterminacy in literature, on transcending the rational, on the evasion of logic, on the end of the tyranny of the author over the reader. No one would publish a sentence of it. Uncle Danny said it was because Leo was blacklisted—but then Uncle Danny thought everything was part of The Conspiracy. "Leo was years, maybe decades, ahead of his time," said my father.

By the time Uncle Leo got to be a century ahead—about 1930, when he was twenty-six—he started coming unglued. He'd always been a fragile web of signs and symbols, absorbing sensations like some vast, skewed telescope scanning a universe of portentous constellations. Now everything fueled his delusions: sounds, colors, the books he'd read. He could believe simultaneously that he was a Dostoyevsky character, Dostoyevsky himself and a man reading about Dostoyevsky. He came to think his mother might be the Grand Inquisitor.

My father said this was when his mother began to be afraid of Uncle Leo.

In the only photo I have of him, Uncle Leo looks fairly benign. He wears gym shorts, a track jersey and a head of hair that falls away from his face in great rich curls like clusters of black grapes. His eyes have a quizzical, questing look. Backlit, his face is framed by his hair and beard, halos around a full moon.

Although he was the second oldest Lidz son, Leo was the closest to Simon. He was a dada's boy whose proclivity for practical jokes came from his old man. Uncle Danny told me that Simon once sat Leo on the corner of Orchard and Stanton streets behind a table on which there was a fishbowl full of water covered by a red velvet cloth. A sign read: ONE PENNY TO SEE THE INVISIBLE FISH. "People got what they paid for," Uncle Danny said.

My father said Uncle Leo had won an award in high school for an essay on citizenship. Eight years later Uncle Harry borrowed the essay and won the contest again. I figured I'd give it a try fifty years later, but by then it had been swallowed up in the black hole of Uncle Arthur's archives.

Uncle Leo told my father he recited classical literature to his high school class—Shakespeare, Shelley, Poe. So the principal asked him to pick a favorite verse to read aloud at an assembly. When Leo took the stage, he said:

> The French, they are a funny race,
> They fight with their feet
> And fuck with their face.

The principal gave Uncle Leo the next three days off to ponder the intricacies of French Literature.

My father loved that story. He told it to me dozens of times.

Uncle Leo endeared himself to his employers the same way. He, too, worked at Borowitz Paint and Wallpaper, whose owners were Fannie's brothers. They gave him a job because they thought they ought to help the family out when Simon died in 1920. The Borowitz brothers were conservative businessmen, closet Republicans. Uncle Leo, on the other hand, used to stand on a stepladder in the store and recite revolutionary poetry. He was a member of the Young People's Socialist League, and played on the Friends of the Soviet Union baseball team. Leo's Red tint started to wear thin on the paint store brothers, who considered subversiveness endemic to the Lidz family.

By 1928 the Borowitz boys were fed up with the Lidzes. They came by to tell Fannie to put her three youngest sons in an orphan's asylum. Uncle Leo, who by now had quit the store, threw his uncles out of the apartment and threw the furniture after them. After that, Uncle Leo withdrew into his room, and Fannie began a daily routine of sliding mail and writing paper beneath his door and leaving meals outside on a tray.

Behind the bedroom door, Uncle Leo wrote notes to remind himself he was not in nineteenth-century Russia, that he was not a nineteenth-century Russian novelist, that he was not a character being pursued in a nineteenth-century Russian novel. He kept writing the notes, but eventually stopped reading them.

One day in 1932 Uncle Leo emerged and decreed himself the Messiah of Washington Heights. He painted a jagged self-portrait that was an unmistakable likeness of Christ. He bragged that the words that flowed from his fingertips could overturn horsecarts in the street. He would make Fannie his Mary Magdalene. He ripped the wedding ring from her hand and jammed it on his own.

"You're crazy," cried Fannie.

"Craziness is holy," screamed Leo.

He grabbed a carving knife and took wild swipes at her. My father, who was then sixteen, tackled him from behind and pinned him to the floor until the police came. Fannie wept, my father wept and Leo wept as he was wrestled into a straitjacket. They took him to Manhattan State Hospital, a high-rise catch basin for the criminally insane. He died at Rockland State Hospital in Orangeburg in 1966. He spent the last thirty-four of his sixty-two years at these two madhouses.

Fannie's sister Lilly was the only Borowitz who visited Leo at Manhattan State. She was so overcome by the filth and cruelty that she never went back. The scene Lilly detailed recalled the bedlam in Hogarth's *The Rake's Progress*: plaster peeling in huge blobs, rotting floors, excrement everywhere. Patients drinking out of spittoons, restrained in straitjackets and leather straps, faces crawling with flies.

Uncle Leo's life in the asylum was a series of assaults on his mind that ran from insulin therapy to electroshock to hydrotherapy, a so-called treatment of immersion in icy water for eight hours. Uncle Danny told me it was "brain fever" that finally killed him.

My mother described Uncle Leo as a sort of dybbuk who lurked in his room by day and prowled through the halls at night. She conjured up a picture of her brother-in-law standing motionless by his door, mumbling and muttering, talking to people no one else could see, gazing into mirrors for hours, hearing voices and seeing demons. But the letters that Uncle Leo sent to my father revealed a cooler, more lucid head, and an ironic sense of humor: During the fifties, when McCarthy and lobotomies were in vogue, he wrote: "I will not have my subconscious cut to fit the current fashion." My father, the great scientist, always talked about Uncle Leo as the Great Writer. He'd say Great Writer with capital letters, as if Great Writers had a Certain Divinity.

I wrote Uncle Leo many letters. He never wrote back, though every Christmas he sent me a keychain he made at the asylum, the same braided plastic keepsake I later learned to assemble at summer camp. He sent my father swatches of poems, occasional entries from his diary, and pages torn from *National Geographic*. He had no doubt his writings would be published some day. He planned to promote them with book safaris down the Amazon and into the Congo. "It's somewhat tiresome," he wrote, "to be alive in the time of your own legend."

But Uncle Leo left the institution only once before he died. The hospital called it "eloping." He and another patient stole a car. A state trooper found him a couple of days later parked in the middle lane of the New York State Thruway.

We met just once, in the back ward of the Orangeburg asylum. It was his sixtieth birthday, and my father and Uncle Danny and Uncle Arthur felt obliged to celebrate the occasion with a visit. I asked to go along. I wanted to ask Uncle Leo about touring Leopoldville, about the invisible fish, about the two holes. My father looked at me for a while and said okay. I felt like I was about to be initiated into a secret lodge.

The day of the visit got off to a depressing start. My father and I drove from Philadelphia to the Bronx to pick up Uncle Arthur and Uncle Danny. We stopped along the way to drop Sandy at the hospital. I had to wear a tie and the paisley sports jacket my mother gave me for sixth-grade graduation. I hated it. It looked like what I saw through the microscope in biology class, and wearing it I felt stiff and tubular, like something ready to be mailed. Later I buried it in the backyard.

My mother, who had now been battling cancer for six years, lay suctioned and plugged, unable to care for herself. She rarely talked, but when she did the oxygen mask made it hard even for my father to know what she said. She communicated by stylus and a Magic Pad. Lift the cellophane cover and the words disappear.

"Short-tempered doctors always lose their patients," my father said as we walked in the door. My mother chuckled softly.

Sandy combed our mother's hair, penciled on eyeliner, rubbed rouge onto her cheeks. Tenderly, intently. "I want you to look good for company," Sandy told her. She patted on face powder. "That's better. Now you don't look sick anymore." But I couldn't take my eyes from the oozing gauze that poked through my mother's gown, or her arms, swollen from hundreds of needle pricks, or her eyes, worn and hollow.

"I told your doctor I hope you're not coming down with that horse disease," said my father.

"I've outgrown all my clothes," Sandy said wistfully.

"He said, 'What horse disease?' "

"Mommy, do you remember the last time we went shopping?"

"I said, 'Bronco Pneumonia.' "

"We had lunch together in that department store."

"He said, 'I hate to make off-the-cough remarks . . .' "

"That was so much fun. When you get better, I want to do it again."

" '. . . but this is a horse of a different cholera.' "

My father and Sandy continued to drift, each alone, sitting together, beside my mother's bed.

Their voices got softer and softer until the room was filled with low murmurings. I watched my mother's gaze shift from him to her to me to the window. The tops of trees were visible, but mostly the window framed the sky. The sky was flat and gray.

"Time to go get Danny and Arthur," my father said.

I stood quietly for a moment in the silence of the room, looking at my mother. With tubes emanating from her body and Sandy's makeup job on her face, she looked frightful. I took her hand and tried to say goodbye, but couldn't speak. I wanted to lean down to kiss her cheek, but couldn't move.

My mother saw the horror in my eyes and squeezed my hand in a way I remembered from sometime long ago. "Now I'm the one in the cloud," she wrote on her Magic Pad.

My mother, the hand.

Rain splattered against the windshield in treacly lumps. My father began one of his endless monologues, just a chant to hold back the darkness. I'd brought the tape recorder to preserve the historic meeting with Uncle Leo, but out of boredom I flipped it on during the drive. Replayed today, my father's words sound rambling and clotted enough to land him in an asylum as well. "Lay psychoanalysis is better left to infertile chickens," he says. "Amateurs who try to find and fix the mental kinks in themselves tend to worry small points and go around in circles. The subconscious is a tricky little device, and the average amateur or even trained psychiatrist can't easily discern which defense mechanism he's encountering: projection, rationalization, repression, substitution. . . . You might say, Who cares? as long as the victim-slash-patient believes in the possibility of correctness of the not-necessarily-accurate given advice. But I suspect the subconscious demands truth. Of course, if the truth hurts, you may have to see a dentist. He'll drill you on the particulars or the bicuspids, depending on whether . . ."

We picked up my uncles in the Bronx, and they sat in the back, Arthur unmoving, Danny—fresh out of Bellevue—restless, unsettled, shifting his shoulders inside his suit, looking back to see if we were being followed. I sat up front, equally uncomfortable in my jacket. I watched the red lights of the tape recorder jitterbug every time my father spoke. I watched the gray afternoon rain spout through the trees. I kicked distractedly at the floorboards. The windshield wipers raced to the beat of *hurry up, hurry up, hurry up*. The popcorn I'd bought at the hospital ran out long before my father's discourse. In desperation, I sucked on burnt kernels.

"Uncle Danny, did you see the rhinoceros?"

"See it? Why wouldn't I see it? What am I, blind?"

Inside the asylum, a young doctor in a white lab coat greeted us with a great, sighing "Hiiiii," flashing a wide, sincere smile he doubtless learned at medical school. My father, the great explainer, presented his opinion: Uncle Leo had a manic-depressive personality. "His symptoms," my father said, "include deep and psychotic depressions, moments of great elation and poor judgment, and periods of delusions of both grandeur and persecution."

The doctor could hardly do anything but nod approval: "And perhaps aggressive-repressive syndrome," he added. He and my father chatted confidently, offering the same diagnoses that had left Uncle Leo without hope of cure for three decades.

Though I was only twelve, I understood that they had no idea what was wrong with Uncle Leo. Uncle Danny's explanation seemed to make just as much sense. According to him, Uncle Leo had drunk a bottle of "Milk of Amnesia."

My own idea of crazy was pretty much based on a Woody Woodpecker cartoon. Woody goes cuckoo when Andy Panda puts salt on his tail, grounding him.

"I can't fly!" squawks Woody. "I can't fly!"

"Fly! Woodpeckers can't fly!" chorus the woodpecker orderlies who fly off with him.

The doctor took us into a patients' lounge. It was a big, empty space, about the size of a basketball court in a high school gym. Strange people were scattered around the room, scouts and sentries on the frontiers of reality.

"What are they waiting for?" asked Uncle Danny.

I looked out a window and saw a yard and a bench and a grassy lane running between a row of trees. I saw a crow lift off and fly over a building. The sky was as flat and gray as it had been when I looked out the window of my mother's hospital room.

The asylum was very noisy. I heard a phonograph needle skipping over the same groove. I could make out somebody playing a scratchy violin somewhere, I listened to the wailing and keening of a woman who looked like she put on her makeup without a mirror. I heard a bamboo flute playing "A Bicycle Built for Two."

> Daisy, Daisy,
> Give me your answer, do.
> I'm half-crazy,
> All for the love of you.

The inhabitants of this dayroom seemed a lot more than half crazy to me. An oily, greasy man who looked like a cockroach ready to slip under the floorboards curled his hair around his finger again and again. Next to him on a folding chair sat the flute player, looking gray and sepulchral. He was as tall as an obelisk, thick as a tombstone. An elderly woman scurried over to me when she saw me staring. "He's really not a flute player," she said. "It's just something he has in his head. He used to live with his family, and they're all *tiny*." The music stopped and the flute player got up and sat on the floor directly in front of us. "Welcome to Leo Lidz's interment," said Uncle Leo. I recognized him then. He looked like my father, but grown old and pale and resigned.

He took off his shoes and invited us to do the same. I did and so did Uncle Arthur. Uncle Danny wouldn't part with anything. "Not me," my father said.

We all joined Uncle Leo on the gray linoleum, beneath the gray ceiling, between gray-brick walls. I studied Uncle Leo. He was a bit more knobby under the chin and creased at the arch of the eyes, but not much heavier than he was in his track star picture. He wore a burgundy watch cap and a shirt that looked as if it had been cut from an early Cubist canvas. Stringy white hair fringed his jaw. His eyes were filled with an old, old knowledge.

I think of him now as a kind of shaman, an ecstatic medicine man in touch with some other world. His magical aura was heightened when he played his flute, with its pure, limpid, incongruous sound. But even when he put it down, and the asylum's air of sad befuddlement swept over him, he remained sharp and somehow attentive.

"Leo, it's you!" said my father.

"It is? Then who are *you*?"

"Who am I? Who *am* I?"

"So you were wondering, too?"

"I'm your brother!"

"I never forget a face," Uncle Leo said, searching

my father's eyes. "But in your case, I'll make an exception."

He pulled in a long breath and tilted his cap at a sassy angle.

"Leo!" my father said, feeding him a straight line from out of his youth. "Tell us about the time you made out in the back of a taxicab."

"Sidney! I didn't invite you here to talk about my checkered career." Uncle Leo, too, enjoyed cranking out puns, particularly at my father's expense. But crazed or uncrazed, the Lidz brothers didn't turn their phrases very far from one another.

There was an awkward silence. Uncle Danny turned to me and, eyeing the pimples that spotted my face, said, "What's that? A disease?" Leo stopped him with a raised palm. Grateful, I offered him a chunk of the halvah from the shopping bag of provisions my father had sneaked in. When Uncle Leo took it from my hand, I saw tears form in his eyes. Uncle Danny later told me halvah was the great treat their father would buy for them long ago on the Lower East Side. I felt Uncle Leo saw me as a real person in that brief moment. I looked at him. He looked at me. His mouth formed words. No sounds came out. I waited. He turned to my father. "They say language is used more for talking than any other," he said. "Don't you think?"

Throughout that long afternoon we sat encrypted in Uncle Leo's world, listening as he capered through a maze of outdated gossip, manic insights and messianic visions. "The kind of commitment and sacrifice the literary life requires made me un-employable," said Uncle Leo, his voice fluttering like a kite. He hadn't had a job in thirty-five years. His life had lapsed into a kind of regulated storage.

He liked to hang around words to see what they said. "Time passes here with inexorable relentless-ness," he told us. "Or is it relentless inexorability?" His conversation was laced with wit, but he often closed his eyes, dropping his head in silent thought for minutes at a time before resuming an idea or an explanation. He rambled on about how his doctors had insisted he kill President Johnson by planting a bomb in the White House. If he didn't, they said, he'd never be released. So Uncle Leo said he slipped into the White House and left a Molotov cocktail under a ladies' room sink.

I thought it sounded neat enough to be true.

"So why didn't President Johnson die?" I asked.

"Because he never used the ladies' room," said Uncle Leo.

Uncle Arthur shook his head. "You shouldn't have to kill the president to get out of a mental hospital," he complained.

Uncle Leo then sat on top of a chest of drawers edged in a kind of rainbow stucco of dried oil paints. He lectured about a conceptual art. No paint, no canvas, no frame. He called it "space-shaping." He described an early composition, which consisted of a single nail hammered into a wall. "Leo Lidz," Uncle Leo said to my father, "called it Proto-Plastic Art. It forced the viewer to visualize all the possibilities for himself. It prevented the artist from fogging up the work with his own conceits."

Uncle Leo continued by telling us his art took on political overtones: "I began to make artistic statements," he said. He used rusty nails. He perfected his technique. He drove the nails farther and farther into the walls until they disappeared. He talked about himself in the third person. "The petite bourgeoisie clamored to buy Leo Lidz's creations," he said. "They realized how practical his art was. It could be hung just about anywhere."

I wanted to laugh. I had to bite my cheeks. My father shot me a sharp look. He wasn't about to laugh and didn't want to be subverted by me. A crazy person, he thought, was incapable of making a joke.

But Uncle Leo was determined. After outlining his painting career, he began relating his exploits in the genre of film. He admitted he'd only made one movie, *Nothing Doing*—without a camera. His technique, he explained, was to expose the film on the locations where the scenes unfolded, producing what he called the "white screen effect."

Uncle Leo had even taken the trouble to write his own review. The film, after all, played only in the Loew's 42nd Street of his mind. I still have the original review, which looks like it was written on a scrap of grocery bag. It remains the only unearthed remnant of Uncle Leo's works. The rest lie buried in Uncle Arthur's archives.

"Visually, the film was pleasing," the reviewer read, "even at times striking, but not particularly imaginative. The cinematography, though skillful, seemed uninspired. The acting was skillful, even, at times, inspired, but not particularly informed. . . ."

My father reacted to this recitation with a whole repertoire of antsy facial movements. His brow crooked, his lips tightened, his teeth clenched.

Uncle Leo went on: "The score, though striking, seemed unimaginative. Technically, the film was pleasingly informed, but not pleasantly inspired. . . ."

My father's body slumped, twisted.

"The dialogue, though strikingly skillful, was not skillfully striking. . . ."

My father was uncomfortable on the floor. He stood up, he arched his back, his knees buckled. His hands moved constantly, open and closed, clamped and spread.

"Though flat, and at times sophomoric and dismal, it was an astonishing work. A little pretentiousness based on a lot of ignorance."

Uncle Leo folded up the tattered piece of bag. He gave it to my father, who stuffed it in his pants pocket along with an assortment of phone numbers, dates, appointments. Most of my father's notes to himself were erased by dry cleaning, but the review survived. He gave it to me later that summer.

Uncle Leo took us to the arts and crafts corner of the room, where he worked sporadically on an easel. He painted by dipping his index finger into a glass of watercolor, hopping on one foot across the floor and slashing at the easel with his finger. He hopped back and forth over and over until the image of a long, stalky man emerged from the thick skein of brown lines as a jacquard pattern appears from the web of yarn on a loom. Uncle Leo stepped back, turned and peered at his painting from another angle and thrust his finger at the image.

"So there he is," he said, "old and forgotten and doing watercolors in a sink."

"Pretty profound," my father remarked sarcastically. Then I realized what I found so strange about my father's behavior. He was still feeling competitive with his brother, even though his brother was a madman.

Uncle Leo went on blithely. "The canvas represents the subconscious id," he told us, "the paint, the ego, the absence of a brush, the superego."

My father sneered. "And what about the easel?"

"The easel," Uncle Leo replied dryly, "is a wooden frame that supports the canvas."

My father stared uncomfortably at the floor. Uncle Danny stared uncomfortably over his shoulder. Uncle Arthur stared at my shoelaces. I stared at Uncle Leo. Uncle Leo stared at himself staring at himself staring at himself.

The slow drip, drip, drip of a faucet marked the time. "I bet Sidney could fix that sink," said Uncle Arthur. "He's got a mechanical mind."

"I know," said Uncle Leo. "I hear the gears squeaking." He laughed, or at least began to. There was a quick breath in his nose—*shshhh*—the first sound of what became, with most adults, a chuckle. With Uncle Leo, that's where the chuckle stopped.

Uncle Arthur was fumbling through a pile of magazines on the floor. He picked out a dozen copies of *Collier's* and *The Saturday Evening Post* he thought suitable for his collection and asked Uncle Leo if he could have them.

"Sure," said Uncle Leo.

My father told Uncle Arthur he couldn't bring them into the car.

Uncle Leo slowly began to sing a song:

> This world is full of foolish facts
> I'm sure you will agree,
> So I just put them all in rhyme
> And learned this melody.
> Foolish facts, foolish facts,
> Foolish things and silly acts,
> But we have nothing else to do
> So let's go crazy.

The violin scratched behind him. The woman with the blotchy makeup left a snakey stream of pee on the linoleum. An orderly followed her with a mop. I remembered wondering if I should tell Uncle Leo I hoped he'd get better soon so he could go home. But where would home have been for Uncle Leo?

Eventually, Uncle Leo got up and walked over to

a window. He reached into his pants pocket and brought out a handful of peanuts and a string. I watched as he tied a nut to the end of the string, then tossed it through the window bars. A squirrel appeared on the ledge and took his bait. I was delighted. Uncle Leo reeled in the squirrel, untied the nut, and with grave and silent pleasure, set the little creature free. Ezra Pound, I later learned, had played a similar game at St. Elizabeth's.

"Something funny's going on around here," said Uncle Danny.

"Really?" said Uncle Leo. "I haven't heard a laugh yet."

Four squirrels played the peanut game. Uncle Leo had named them, just as Simon had named the moths in his basement. The biggest he called Ivan, after the morose Karamazov brother. "Ivan's perfectly content here," Uncle Leo said. "What squirrel wouldn't love to live in a nuthouse? Oh my!, Oh no! Hoho! Heehee! Ha! Ha! Ha! Ha!"

That bleating woodpecker laugh coming from this knobby, stony, sepulchral man made me realize for the first time he might truly be crazy.

Next Uncle Leo began reading his latest work: "The pimply and hairy skin rushing over the collar's edge . . . under black fur hood . . . grnnh! rrnnh, pthg . . . revives my spirits opens my pores . . . addressing crowds through their arse holes . . . a furred tail upon nothingness . . . chut chut chut . . . arms shrunk into fins . . ."

He read on as if we were the students at a Washington Heights high school convocation.

". . . square even shoulders and the satin skin . . . faces smeared on their rumps . . ."

Uncle Leo paused, he sighed, he squinted at the text, he took his glasses off and cleaned them on his shirt tail, he swiped sweat off his brow with his sleeve, he rebaited his string, he ignored my father's annoyed tapping.

". . . for all her naked beauty, bit not in tropic skin . . . stone in his bladder . . ."

Uncle Arthur fell asleep on his chair by the window where the squirrel had appeared. Uncle Danny and my father sat together on the radiator, crossing and uncrossing their legs in unison like a two-man drill team. People left the day room, and new people came in. Nothing else changed much. Somebody turned on the lights.

I whispered, "Is this what being crazy means, Dad?"

He explained Uncle Leo had culled a collage of references to skin and fur from Pound's *Cantos*. He said it matter-of-factly, as if all twelve-year-olds knew who Pound was.

"Leo calls it *A Pound of Flesh*," he said.

Uncle Leo read on and on until my father finally stopped him for the little ceremony he had planned. My father brought out the champagne and cake he'd concealed in his shopping bag. Somewhere between the black fur and the bladder, I'd stuck half-a-dozen candles into the frosting.

Uncle Leo asked Uncle Danny to light one in honor of their mother. He asked Uncle Arthur to read a birthday poem Uncle Harry had sent from *his* asylum. Uncle Arthur muddled through it in the slow, hesitant way of plain men who rarely say poetry aloud:

> The trains scream to a stop,
> And the toilweary crowd surges in,
> From factory and shop,
> Homeward bound for the night with their kin.
> Hear that chant, all about,
> Sway to it, vacantly
> Clackerty, clickerty,
> Wheels spinning, wheels singing.
> Hopeful hearts, flying on,
> Hearts all dead, grinding on,
> Tearful hearts, tugging on.
> Hearts with hate, roaring on.
> Clackerty, rushing wheels,
> Clickerty, spinning wheels,
> Centuries, warm with love.
> Centuries, cold with fear.
> Hear that chant of life's throb
> Swaying on, year by year.

My uncles were like that, I thought: swaying vacantly above life's clackerty, clickerty spinning wheels.

Uncle Leo snuffed out the candles, leaving a little trail of smoke drifting in the air; as he watched it rise, his face grew dark and deep. He imparted a

portmanteau word from *Finnegan's Wake*: Funferal.
"That's what it is, brothers. Funferal in this funeral."

My father loosened the cork on the champagne.
I could hardly wait for it to pop out and hit the ceiling like it did in Bugs Bunny cartoons, but the con-
tents didn't even fizz. Uncle Arthur pocketed the
cork, and my father filled the glasses. Even I got
one.

"It's not Dom Perignon," my father said, "but it'll
do."

"Do what?" asked Uncle Arthur.

Everyone raised a glass to his lips.

"Here's to Leo," said my father.

"Here's to Harry," said Uncle Danny.

"Here's to the crazy Lidz brothers," said Uncle
Leo.

After the third toast I, too, was feeling the crazy
camaraderie of the Lidz boys. They were all crazy,
I thought. My father included. It seemed very nice
to be crazy. I looked at them and they were smiling
and I smiled with them.

"Let's go take a walk," said Uncle Leo. We followed him across the day room, through a screen
door and out to a grassy knoll under an oak tree.

He read from another clipping as he walked: "A
survey done recently by the town engineer indicates
that the south end of the high school track is a full
five feet lower than the north end, Superintendant
Beats informed the School Committee. 'I knew
there was a slope in the track,' said Beats, 'but I

was surprised it rose that much. Thus, no records can be made on the track.' "

This phenomenon fascinated Uncle Leo. He construed from the article that a runner who circled the course would be ten feet higher than when he started. If he ran a second lap, he'd be twenty feet higher.

"Impossible!" my father said testily.

"Nothing is impossible," said Uncle Leo, "although improbability is possibly possible. The impossible is probably improbable, but probably not impossible. What interests me about this track is that it *is* impossible.

"As Superintendant Beats has made clear, the more you run on the course, the longer you have to. You can stop, but you can't ever finish. It's the same with the ocean: The deeper you swim, the nearer to the surface you'll be." Then, in a Chaplinesque burlesque, he crumpled up the clipping, tossed it over his shoulder and kicked it away with his heel.

Clouds massed in the sky as evening approached. I was getting chilly. Uncle Leo flashed something from beneath his shirt. I never found out what it was. Something bloody and sinister, I thought. I always wondered if it was the head of a squirrel. Now I think it was only a reflection of the expectations of madness that adults thrust on a child.

We left Uncle Leo revolving on the Mobius orbit of his life. He shambled off, slow and rickety but with a strange formal dignity. One thing he said that day stays with me still: "Sidney, I'm not all I'm cracked up to be." As I think back, I hear a preacher, an actor, a three-card monte dealer, a professor, an anarchist, a brother, my uncles, my father.

Chapter 8

The Dance of Elimination

I was surrounded by the loud hum of people talking. They seemed to want something from me; I didn't know what. I wished I were invisible, like one of Uncle Leo's fish.

The rabbi came up to where I was standing in the living room, took my hand and wrung it. "She was a wonderful woman," he whispered in my ear. "She was a wonderful woman." His words swam around in my head and I thought, "Who *will* make my lunch?"

This was as difficult for him as it was for me, the rabbi said. I knew he was lying.

I was led to the kitchen by someone I'd seen in the audience at my Bar Mitzvah, a white-faced man wearing a toupee that moved at a different tempo than he did. "Take deep breaths. Through your mouth," Aunt Joanie instructed while she knotted my tie. Aunt Bobbye told me to smile and drink some soda. I tried to do both but couldn't: I was too busy breathing. So I alternately breathed and smiled and sipped. I felt like I was underwater.

I leaned against the refrigerator in my blue-green iridescent suit. It hadn't been out of the closet since my Bar Mitzvah, three months earlier. My mother's brother-in-law Bob, the soap salesman, said, "Stand up straight, please, and stop biting your nails." I stiffened and jammed one hand in my pocket. I held the glass of soda in the other. Now I was stiff, breathing, smiling, sipping.

My father looked as lost as I was. His shirt was a riot of wrinkles, his pants sagged away from his knees, even his hair looked confused. A thin smile had remained on his face all morning. Whoever told him to smile forgot to remind him to stop.

"Sid, you ought to cover all the mirrors."

"Sid, you ought to buy the kids a dog."

"Sid, you ought to hide all the pictures of Selma."

I ran to the living room to claim a picture of my mother before my father could hide them all. The one I snatched showed her standing with Sandy on our lawn out on Long Island. Sandy was a baby, maybe two or three, tugging at my mother's hand. Sandy pulled and pulled, dragging her into my father's photo, but my mother remained unmoved, looking harried and a bit impatient.

This day Sandy tagged after my aunts, wailing. She had been that way since my father told her. He didn't have to tell me. I'd been playing football in Jay Herman's backyard when the phone call came. Jay's mother, Flossie, had waved me into the house. "Your father is coming to pick you up," she told me. I knew then my mother was dead because Flossie didn't say another word to me.

I went out front and stood on the curb and watched for my father's car, hoping he would never come. But his old, bruised Chevy came down the cold road and stopped. He waited until I got in the car before saying, "Your mother died this morning." I resisted hearing him with my whole body. I wanted to shrink away and at the same time I wanted to smash out the window. I wanted to get out of the car and run and run and run.

My father didn't say anything else on the short drive home. I looked at him surreptitiously, but he looked straight ahead. I couldn't speak and he couldn't speak. Our love for my mother had made us dumb.

Sandy was on the porch when we drove up. She had come home to find my aunts bustling around the house. She thought they were making a coming-home party for my mother.

She ran happily to the car.

"Aunt Bobbye and Joanie are here!" she said innocently. "Are you going to get Mommy?"

My father took Sandy's hand, walked up to the front steps with her and sat her next to him. I didn't want to see any more. I felt tight and twisted inside, a cable caught in an awful wind.

Then I heard my sister: "No! No! No!"

I had listened to Sandy's denial and felt as helpless and unraveled as Uncle Arthur.

Uncle Arthur and Uncle Danny had immediately

come down from the Bronx to sit shiva, honoring the dead in the traditional Jewish way. Now Uncle Arthur was standing in the living room, a mute monitor in the babble of people. I drifted in from the kitchen and stood beside him.

"How's the garbage, Arthur?" asked Aunt Joanie's husband, Bob. He came into focus out of the crowd near the coffee table.

"It's not garbage, it's junk."

"Has it changed much over the years?"

"There's just more of it."

"Why do you save that shit, Arthur?"

"What do you think of people who go to the movies and have a good time? Do you think they're all OK? Everybody's a little off the ticker."

Aunt Joanie and Aunt Bobbye joined us.

"Smile," Aunt Joanie said.

"Stand straight," Uncle Bob said.

"Eat something, you'll feel better," Aunt Bobbye said.

Nobody bossed Sandy around. They couldn't. She ricocheted around the living room, howling her grief in great awesome gulps, unconsoled by the constant buzz of too many adults. Her shoulders had caved in and her mouth looked bruised. She chewed away at her nails. Her fingertips were raw. She cried, wiped her eyes, and cried again. Her face was splotchy. "Why . . . did . . . Mommy . . . die?" The words came in heaving gasps. "Why? . . . Why? . . . Why?" I wished she would shut up.

Uncle Arthur moved into the living room to comfort Sandy, but she clung to Aunt Joanie, frightened by his pale, dry, cadaverous presence. He turned toward me and I hugged him, his frail body a bundle of sticks in my arms. We sat down together on the couch, so close I could feel his angular body.

"Was it horrible when your mother died?" I asked him, pushing the words past the sharp stone of sorrow in my throat.

"Maybe. Yeah. I don't know. I think so. Yeah."

He stared at his shoes. I looked, too. They were scuffed and splayed. "My mother died in the night," Uncle Arthur said in the slow, painful way he spoke when he pulled memories from the hidden caverns of his heart. "She had a tooth pulled that day and it made her very weak. She died with her mouth open. It upset me a little bit."

"That her mouth was open?"

"No, no. Her dying. I didn't like it much, but—I don't know—I always kept myself busy with a lot of things. It makes you forget a little."

"What about Uncle Danny?"

"After she died, Danny got sick and couldn't get out of bed. I had to say prayers in synagogue for him. For three weeks. He'd get neck aches and dizzy spells and I had to wrap a rag with lemon-something around his head. He lay in bed, repeating our mother's name: Fannie, Fannie, Fannie. He'd look at the plaster on the ceiling and watch the shapes."

"What shapes?"

"Lips, lips. He looked up and saw my mother's

mouth. He didn't want to eat or drink or sleep until he saw her soul leave her mouth. His mouth was wide open, but I couldn't get any food in. He said it hurt too much. I think he hurt on account of our mother."

"You didn't hurt?"

"It wasn't *my* mouth."

"I mean, you didn't cry?"

"No, no."

"But Uncle Danny did."

"Yeah."

"What made him stop?"

"I said, 'Danny, cut it out.' I said, 'Get yourself together.' I said, 'You need a hobby, like collecting.' So he got a hobby—his religion. That's the only thing he liked. He prayed every morning and every night. And, believe it or not, that's what pulled him out."

Uncle Danny came across the room with a sure, but careful step and handed me a prayer book. I stood up, holding Uncle Arthur's hand. Uncle Danny bowed toward Jerusalem and said the prayers that begin the minyan. People stopped talking as he mumbled through the Kaddish. His breathy singsong was as soothing as the lines and folds and callouses in Uncle Arthur's hand. My father sadly joined him toward the end, intoning the ancient words for the dead.

Sandy whimpered in counterpoint to the Hebrew words of mourning. I reached out and drew her to me. "You're OK," I said. "It'll be all right. Get yourself together." Her tears stopped. Everyone looked at me, the heroic big brother. I felt like an idiot.

"Sandy," Uncle Danny said, "you're the mother of the house now."

Her temporary composure evaporated. "Mommy! Mommy! Mommy!" she shrieked, and bolted into the circle of adults. Her reddish-brown hair bobbed and disappeared into the mass of dark, funereal suits and black dresses.

"For God's sake, Danny!" said my Aunt Bobbye. "She's having a hard enough time. Can't you be more sensitive?"

Uncle Danny took my hand. "Come on, *kidela,* let's leave these yentas alone."

We withdrew to the den. Uncle Arthur, silent again, followed us. The dark room and Uncle Danny's cigarette and Uncle Arthur's old paper smell made me feel safe. I turned on the television. Onscreen Daffy Duck was being tormented by a whimsical, unseen cartoonist who kept changing the background from farmland to Arctic tundra to tropical jungle until the duck's world became white blankness. "I've never been so humiliated in all my life," Daffy croaked. Uncle Danny bobbed his head in sympathetic anger. The cartoonist erased Daffy's body, daubed him with stripes and polka dots and hoisted a banner from his tail. Its crest was a screw and a ball. Battered, abased and blown apart, Daffy finally said, "All right—enough is enough. This is the final, this is the very, very last straw. . . . Who is responsible for this? I demand that you show your-

self! Who are you? Huh!" The cartoonist drew a
door and banged it shut on Daffy. The camera
pulled away to reveal Daffy's creator: Bugs Bunny.

I laughed and looked at Uncle Danny, who was
up and doing an apache war dance.

"Dirty rabbit bastard!" Uncle Danny roared.

My father slammed into the room. "Shut up,
Danny," he said. "Don't you have *any* sense of pro-
priety? We're sitting shiva and you're screaming at a
fucking cartoon!"

Uncle Danny looked at him with sharpening dis-
gust. "That spiteful Hitler rabbit's erasing the Jews,
and you want me to shut up! Erasing the Jews and
you don't see it? You don't see it!"

My father melted away before Uncle Danny's
burning paranoia.

Someone tapped at the window. It was Ash.

I went over, opened the window and leaned out.
"Where have you been?" I asked.

"At a taffy pull in a leper colony."

He had been unwelcome at our house since my
Bar Mitzvah party. He'd grabbed Aunt Joanie's am-
ple breasts from behind and held on like a monkey
on a racehorse. My father had to pry him loose.

Ash had showed up to pay back the fall I'd just
taken for him. He had scribbled "Bambino Bruno
bears big bulbous boobs" on a page of my looseleaf
notebook. I tore off the message, put it on Bambino's lunch tray and waited with Ash for her to dis-
cover it. She did and took it to the principal, who
began a schoolwide investigation. He found the

other half of the page in a trash can. My name was doodled on it. I was called into his office.

"Do you know who wrote this?"

"It wasn't me."

"Whoever did has a really perverted mind."

I shrugged and remained loyal to Ash. I refused to fink.

I was suspended from school. My mother grounded me for a month. She was already confined to her bed, so she made *me* fetch my father's leather belt. "Turn around and drop your pants." I refused. "Turn around!" I bent over. She snapped the strap at me three times ineffectually. She was very weak. I went back to my room and as I lay on the floor, staring at the swirling planets, I wished she was dead. Now she was, and I thought of all the other things I could have wished for.

"Let's go," Ash said.

"Where?"

"The Troc. We can still catch the matinee."

"I can't go to the Troc. My mother's dead."

"It'll be fun."

"I don't know. My Mom's dead."

"Come on."

"You mean the strip joint?"

"What other Troc is there, stupid?"

"I'll never get in."

"Don't worry. I'll take care of everything."

"But how are we gonna get there?"

"I said I'll take care of everything."

Ash had his mother's car.

He serenaded me with dead mother jokes all the way downtown. "Get your dog yet? Or is your Uncle Danny enough?"

The Troc was smack in the middle of the Philadelphia tenderloin, a tattersall of porn movies, pawnshops and seedy hotels. On the shady side of the street, the old grindhouse loomed ahead of us like the cover of a dirty book. I looked at all this grime—dingy arches, filthy columns—and didn't want to go in. Even the bulbs in the marquee over the box office made more shadows than light. I thought of old guys in a toilet. I thought of my uncles' Bronx apartment.

Ash bought us tickets and handed me mine. He sailed straight ahead, leaving me to figure out how to get past the guy at the door on my own. The ticket taker looked a little like my principal, only meaner. I pushed my right foot forward and my left caught on a broken tile. I turned my head. I hunched my shoulders. I stood on tiptoes and inched past the doorman. He took my ticket without even looking at me.

"Let's hit the balcony," Ash said.

The balcony smelled like some awful combination of a urinal and the bottom of my gym locker. I sat next to a worn guy in a worn football jersey. I didn't know where to put my elbows: Ash couldn't bear to be touched, and I certainly didn't want to touch the football jersey.

Ash began to bray at the stripper. He was the only vital sign in the joint. Cella Fane, the See-

Through Girl, had come onstage to perform the Dance of Elimination. I thought maybe I ought to leave or at least turn my head. But I couldn't. Ash would have thought I was a jerk, and besides, he had the car. I was all sweaty. My shoes stuck to the floor. I wondered if I was supposed to get a hard-on.

"E-lim-in-*a*-tion," the MC declaimed. "Now as Noah Webster—he's the boy who wrote the dictionary—said, elimination means to take off, to discard, to throw away, to cast off. . . ." Cella Fane took off her gloves, discarded her stiletto heels, threw away her stockings and cast off her gold-sequined gown. When everything was eliminated, she did some calisthenics we hadn't yet gotten to at Welsh Valley Junior High.

"It's the Oriental Muscle Dance," said Ash.

Cella Fane had a cheerfully ugly face and a body like a second helping of mashed potatoes. Twin tarantulas were glued to her breasts. I thought I could see little bits of hair peeking out of the triangle that covered her crotch. She seemed as bored as a countergirl slapping bologna into a hoagie roll at the Reading Terminal. This lumpy mashed-potato lady suddenly looked a lot like Nanny Ruth, who'd had a stroke two years before. I had been in Aunt Bobbye's house and seen Nanny Ruth wander the rooms naked and insane, her face stained with mascara. Cella Fane was as embarrassing to look at as Nanny Ruth. I wondered why I had a hard-on.

The procession of strippers had names my father could have thought up: Emma Nems, Anna Cyn, Takya Vestoff, Carlotta Tendant, Bermuda Schwartz. All this delighted Ash, who bounced up and down in his seat like a tassel on Cella Fane's G-string.

"What are you doing?" I asked.

"Jerking off, you jerkoff."

"What?"

"I'm gonna come in this popcorn cup. Then I'm gonna dump it on the creeps downstairs."

I flinched, as if he'd dropped ice cubes down my pants.

"You do it, too," he said.

"I don't want to beat a good thing to death."

"Come on."

"I don't think I can pull it off."

"Are you chicken?"

"Things could get out of hand."

"You sound like your fucking father."

He was right and I knew it. The more cornered I felt, the more I sounded like my father. I could hear in my voice the hysterical puns he used to avoid confrontation of any kind.

Ash passed me the empty cup. "Fill it up," he said. "The men's room is down the stairs."

When I opened the door, I checked for hidden cameras and banged on the mirror to see if it was two-way. I smiled, stood up straight and breathed deeply through my mouth. Then I threw up.

Ten minutes later I emerged. "Not tonight," I said. "I've got a headache."

"Don't tell me about your shortcomings," Ash said. He was annoyed. He got up to leave. I followed. On the way back he careened all over the expressway, sometimes steering with his feet. A sparrow swooped in a low arc and smashed against the windshield, covering the glass with feathers and blood. "Dead bird, dead bird, dead bird," Ash yelled.

We drove by Benji Kessle's house.

"Let's blow up his mailbox," said Ash.

"With what?"

"I'll take care of it."

He handed me an M-80. "I'll wait in the car," he said. "You light it." I lit the fuse, sprinted to the mailbox and hurled in the M-80. The firecracker went off with a thump and twisted the mailbox into a tangle of aluminum.

"We did it, Ash!" I shouted.

The car roared off and I stood there, once again the fool, listening to a snatch of Ash's laughter.

The lights came on in the house and through one of the windows I could see Benji sitting with his mother at the dining room table. Benji came to the door.

I dropped down into the ditch by the mailbox and pressed my face into the earth. I didn't want anyone to see me anymore.

Chapter 9

Safety in Numbers

The second time I thought about running away from home I packed the gifts Uncle Arthur bestowed on me for my Bar Mitzvah: a dog bowl and a dozen of what he called his lucky bucks.

"Every time I dream about finding a dollar on the sidewalk," he told me, "the next day I find one." Each bill was marked with the time and place of discovery.

"What the hell's he going to do with a dog bowl?" my father had asked.

"It's a good eating bowl," said Uncle Arthur. "And it won't tilt."

Once again Uncle Arthur's innocence was prescient. His turned out to be the most useful off all my Bar Mitzvah gifts.

As Ash predicted, we got a dog, but not until my parakeet died. One Saturday morning I found Chunky dead on the bottom of his cage, stiff, his little stick feet in the air like the hands of a tiny beggar.

My father took one look at me and said, "Let's go

buy a dog." Walking around among the pens at the pound, I recoiled from the hundreds of puppies pawing and frisking at the chicken wire. They were yelping, pathetic, demanding creatures. "Here's a boxer," my father said. He liked a trim, tidy, self-confident dog. But I was drawn, finally, to the one in the next cage. He was biscuit-colored, half German Shepherd, half collie. His body was stooped and apologetic, but he had smart eyes. The sign on his cage said his name was King.

"Why do you want him?" my father asked. "He's already full grown."

"I don't know," I said. "I just like him."

Sandy put down the puppy she was cuddling and looked King over. "I like him, too," she decided. "But I don't like his name."

We brought King home and, after a family pow-wow, renamed him Clyde. Uncaged, he was stubborn and independent and a good friend. I took him for walks that were never long enough; he had to be dragged back to the house. Sometimes he'd light out the door and be gone for days, only to return with an offering: a bird, a branch, an inner tube. Once he left a bloody heap of moles on the doorstep.

We'd sit together by the sweet gum tree and looked down at the road that passed by our house. I told him things; his doleful, red-rimmed eyes filled with canine understanding. My mother had been dead just two months, but it was if she had disappeared from our lives. Eventually, my father uncovered the mirrors, but her pictures were never brought out again. He never mentioned her, and neither did I. It wasn't just her absence—I didn't have the expectation she would come back—but more; I felt as if something had been cut away from me, like an amputee who still feels twinges in his lost leg.

My father tried frantically to fill in for my mother the only way he knew: by numbers. He wrote out schedules, duty rosters, marching orders. His alarm went off every morning at six forty-five. I listened as he ran in place, then counted off sets of jumping jacks and sit-ups and Marine Corps pushups. "Ten minutes and fifty-two point three seconds today," he said. "Forty-eight years old and I've never been in better condition."

After a four-minute shower, he'd go to his bureau and take out a fresh white shirt. He had unwrapped each shirt and crossed the sleeves in front as if in prayer against disorder. In the kitchen, he fried some eggs, sunny-side up. "Two eggs," he said. "Two perfect eggs." He was pleased more by the aesthetics of the number than the prospect of eating.

I fell gladly into his mathematical mode. On weeknights at five-thirty I turned the oven to four hundred and twenty-five degrees and popped in three chicken pot pies. Sandy set the table at five forty-five. My father arrived at six. We three sat down to eat at six oh-five. At six twenty-five I cleared the table and Sandy washed the dishes.

This routine continued for a month until my father became engrossed in a new project—a tape recorder with an echo reverb—and began coming home later and later.

Sandy never joined in my father's numbers game. She didn't believe in him as a mother. But she kept to the schedule for the first few nights we were alone. Then we quit having dinner at the kitchen table, and ate while watching TV in his bedroom. I would lay on my father's side of the bed, Sandy on my mother's. There were times when she would fall asleep and I would carry her back to her room, but I always waited up for him. He would come in at nine, ten, eleven o'clock, still wanting to talk about his work. We would sit at his desk, where Sandy would set out her idea of a late-night snack: Ritz crackers and Philadelphia cream cheese. A careful eater, my father would spread an equal amount of cheese on each cracker with the same smooth, deft turn of his hand.

"How're you doing at school?" he might absently ask.

"OK," I'd say.

"Good."

Then he'd natter on about tuners and amplifiers and pre-amps, all the components of the hi-fi systems he was working on. Talking wasn't enough. I watched him try to express his ideas with his hands, forming globes and pyramids and geodesic domes. I watched and listened and nodded and nodded.

I often left him sitting at his desk, perhaps fumbling through the figures in his checkbook, a job that had always been my mother's. He would have drowned in medical bills, had she not quietly taken out an insurance policy on herself. She understood my father would never have thought of such a thing. He could only deal with the ordered numbers of the universe, not the unruly ones of human life.

Still, in the first months after my mother's death, he was overtaken by a frenzy of fatherhood. He took us to art museums and electronics conventions and a march on Washington. He took us camping in the Adirondacks and he read us not only Spinoza, but also Pinter, Beckett and the rest of the Theater of the Absurd. "We are all born mad," he told us. "Some of us remain so." On one tape from that period he talks to me as if we were colleagues in the School of Socrates: "My first feelings of rejection of their continual anguish over the absurdity of the human condition is now in the process of reappraisal. These playwrights don't mean 'crazy' by the word absurd, they mean out of harmony with reason; illogical, not ridiculous; 'without purpose' might be a better way to put it. Of course, I can't really accept the concept of a meaningless universe—God or no dog."

I was thirteen years old. The more verbose and convoluted my father became, the more silent and withdrawn I became. I chose my words very prudently, so prudently that sometimes I couldn't say anything at all. My history teacher, for one, stopped asking me questions completely because I took so long to answer him.

School lost its meaning for Sandy altogether. She went to class, she came home, she played with her dolls. Even now I can hear my sister talking to them, her voice floating small and feathery from her room. My father would ask if he could help her with her schoolwork. "I don't have any," she'd say. Sandy's teachers lost patience, and her grades slipped deeper and deeper into the alphabet.

I had to let my father help me. I couldn't hold him back. When I was assigned to write a dramatic scene for English class, he suggested a satire on the home life of Jesus, Mary and Joseph. It seemed funny to me, but my English teacher found it blasphemous. She didn't object so much to Jesus as a beatnik or Mary as an adulteress with God, but my father's one joke outraged her. In the gospel according to Sidney Lidz, Jesus complained: "With a name like Jesus, everybody thinks I'm Puerto Rican."

My English teacher read it and sent me to the principal, the same one who called me a pervert. This time he told me not to return to school without a note from my father.

My father composed an appeal as if I were going before a Supreme Court of the Absurd. He showed me the final draft:

Jesus is either a concept, a man, a god, a goal, an attitude, etc. Especially etc. Assuming his existence in every year since zero-point-zero A.D., people have written whatever story they chose to make him a god, saint, revolutionary or criminal. I haven't written the book yet—but I'm sure many people have—from the viewpoint of Judas explaining that Jesus was a counterrevolutionary and that's why he was turned in to the fuzz. For example, money changing was necessary when a traveler arrived in town with his "foreign" money. The temple was the true center of life, and this is where you got your local currency. Jesus kicked the money changers out: Maybe he wanted to separate the secular from church activity. Was that good? If I remember correctly from my stolen Gideon hotel bible, the *Letter to the Corinthians* told everyone that because Jesus had done all this great sacrificing work, you no longer had to be circumcised to make your covenant with God. But wouldn't that be antiexistential?

Fortunately, I don't know anything about these things, so I am not required to have an opinion. But I am reading. In the meantime, I ask that you reconsider my son's suspension.

I told him this letter would keep me suspended until I was eighteen.

"Don't be silly," my father said. "It'll work."

I watched the principal read the letter and stare perplexedly into space. He eyed me frostily. He was no existentialist. "What you and your father fail to understand is that this school is not a forum for your iconoclastic beliefs. As an official of this school district, I will in no way tolerate having my students exposed to godlessness. Very rarely do I tell students not to listen to their parents, but I am telling you: This kind of thinking will not get you very far in life. More to the point, since I can find no apology in this note, the suspension will stand."

I was relieved. School seemed pointless. I hadn't made the honor roll since my mother died. I'd just as soon spend the three days home with Clyde.

"The letter didn't work," I said when my father came home that night. "I'm still suspended."

He didn't know what I was talking about. He'd forgotten the whole thing.

My rat-friend Ash had been suspended, too. He'd carved his initials into a biology class turtle, poured lighter fluid over the shell and set it on fire in the woods behind the school. He'd been having a lot of fun this semester, slashing his chewing gum in the hair behind my ear and gluing the pages of my geometry notebook together before an exam. He used the ultraviolet crayons my father had given me to write curse words on the classroom walls. We sat together in English class happy with our secret that the walls were covered with obscenities invisible except under ultraviolet light.

Two days into my suspension, Ash came over to the house wrapped in aluminum foil. He called his outfit a spacesuit. He looked like a space mummy.

"My Mom's getting married again," he said.

"Who to?"

"The guy who owns the new supermarket."

"Do you like him?

"I *hate* him."

"Then why's your mother marrying him?"

"Because he's got money and a big dick."

Ash told me he needed my father's tape recorder with the echo reverb. As I went to get it from the hall closet, he said, "Bring his movie camera, too." We walked through the woods behind my house to the new supermarket, and I shadowed him down the aisles with the Super 8. He began stuffing steaks under the foil.

"Hey, kid," the store manager shouted. "What the fuck are you doing?"

Ash spoke into the reverb. "HEY, KIDDDDD. WHAT THE FUCK ARE YOU DOINNNNNG-GGGG?"

"Do you want me to call the cops?"

"DO YOU WANT ME TO CALL THE COPPP-PSSSS?"

"I don't have to take this shit."

"I DON'T HAVE TO TAKE THIS SHIIIITT-TTT."

The manager saw me filming, laughed and unaccountably walked away.

"What an asshole," Ash said. "He thinks he's on *Candid Camera*."

I filmed Ash all the way out of the supermarket, his glittery foil spacesuit full of porterhouse and sirloin. He began tossing the steaks into the gutter as soon as we got outside. He was laughing, and I laughed along with him, two outlaws in the badlands of the suburban frontier.

We walked home. But then Ash went too far.

In my backyard he tried to tie a cherry bomb to Clyde's tail. My dog! I took off after Ash and brought him down with a blindside tackle. I grabbed Clyde. Ash smacked me in the ear.

"What are you, nuts?" I screamed.

"I want to see how your dog looks in bangs."

"Stop it! Beat it! Come back and I'll punch your face in."

Now I was down to one friend: Clyde.

For the rest of the school year I spent most of my spare time in my room, tossing the sockball against the door. Thud, thud, thud, thud. Clyde watched disinterestedly. Obsessively, I filled composition books with statistics attributed to my make-believe players. Every so often my father would come into my room looking for clean socks. He'd unravel my sockball and leave for the office with my game on his feet.

"Why don't you go up to see Danny and Arthur?" my father asked toward the end of the school year.

"I just don't feel like it," I said.

A few days later he hit me with another idea.

"Mrs. Fredrickson's going west this summer on another two-month trip," he said. "Want to go along?"

"I'd rather stay home with Clyde," I said.

"You'll feel better if you're off by yourself."

Mrs. Fredrickson was a schoolteacher who drove cross-country every June with a minivan full of eighth-graders. Right after school ended, we took

off with three other kids. I remember scenic won-
ders and historic landmarks as a kind of grab bag of
rest stops. Each kid had an assignment; mine was
to tote up the miles every day and figure out how
many we were getting to a gallon of gas. Tabulating
the miles slowly distanced me from my mother's absence.

Sandy stayed home; her grades were so bad she
had to go to summer school. My father briefly liberated himself by going to Grossinger's, but
sprained his ankle the first day playing tennis, and
drove back the second. "I've been mowing the lawn,
fixing the car," he wrote me. "And going on an occasional date with female women."

I looked forward to coming home. I missed
Clyde. I missed Sandy. I missed my father's weird
scientism, his long quotes from Spinoza, even his
absentminded concentration on his work. I wanted
to sit down with my father and astound him with
the geology of the Painted Desert and the Grand
Canyon.

I arrived home early one morning and went in to
find him in his workshop. Before I said a word, he
announced he was taking Sandy and me out for
breakfast. Clyde clambered into the car with us,
and we drove off.

"Where are we going?" Sandy asked.

My father checked his car compass.

"North by northeast," he said.

"*Where* are we going?" I asked.

"Know where?"

"No, where?"

"Nowhere."

His punhouse tour irked me. He hadn't talked to me all summer, and now all I got was wordplay. His puns were like static that confused something I knew he was afraid to say.

"Where?" said Sandy.

"Out for breakfast," he said.

"I'm not hungry," I said. "Let's go back home."

"No, I want you to meet someone."

"Who?"

"Someone you'll really like."

What now? I thought. Meeting someone my father thought I'd "really like" made me suspicious and queasy. As we drove north along Roosevelt Boulevard I looked out the window at the row houses and wondered if I'd like to meet the people who lived in them. We passed street after street of houses that looked as if they'd been built yesterday for people who'd move out tomorrow. The homes thinned out as we drove deeper and deeper into another suburb.

"Where are we going, Dad?" I asked.

"Someplace you'll really have fun."

I didn't like the looks of the split-levels we were driving through now. We lived on a hill. Everything out here was flat.

"What kind of fun, Daddy?" asked Sandy.

"Fun, Sandy, fun. It's a surprise."

Now I was getting really worried. I didn't think

my father could cook up any surprises I thought would be fun anymore.

We turned into a curving road and stopped at a house in the middle of the block. It was big and white with brick siding up to the edge of the picture window in the living room. The lawn was cropped short and bordered by small rows of evergreens. An International Harvester van was in the driveway.

We got out of the car and walked toward the house. I felt like somebody was watching us. Somebody was. The door opened and I saw an upright woman with a tight little smile. Her yellow hair was swept up in a crowning knot. Three nondescript children peered out at us from behind her.

"I'm so happy to meet you children," she said. "Your father has told me all about you."

Who *is* this? I wondered. She acted as if she already knew who we were. Sandy and I had never seen her before. She didn't treat my father like a guest.

My father introduced Shirley. Everything about Shirley—her blouse, her makeup, her boxy orthopedic shoes—was the same exact shade of iron gray. Everything except her skirt, which was gunmetal. Her face was taut and uninviting. Her smile was as fixed and severe as her hair.

"He seems very quiet," Shirley said, looking me over.

"He's just shy."

The living room was outfitted in a style my father

used to ridicule as Philadelphia Jewish Renaissance: gold-flocked wallpaper, gold sculpted carpet and a polished baby grand that looked like it wasn't meant to be played. On the mantel stood two enormous troll dolls, their eyes as lusterless as Shirley's kids'.

"Would you like to help me set the table, Sandy?"

"OK," said Sandy warily.

Shirley put my father at the head of the table. Sandy sat on his left. I was next to her and across from Shirley's kids, who stood gaping at us as if they thought we would juggle the plates. Shirley's place was opposite my father's, but she never did sit down because she was serving pancakes.

"Oh wow, pancakes!" said my father. "Our favorite breakfast."

"He's not eating, Sidney."

"He's not hungry, Shirley."

Why are they talking over my head? I thought. Now I understood what Uncle Danny meant when he talked about the world being full of actors. My father and this vision in gray sounded like they were speaking lines written by someone else. I felt as paranoid as Uncle Danny. Those pancakes might as well have been poison.

Sandy passed out napkins and poured the orange juice. "Good girl, Sandy," Shirley said. "I can tell you'll make a terrific helper around the house."

"A fork and a teaspoon sat on the table," my father said.

"The fork said: 'Who was that ladle I saw you

with last night?" The spoon replied, 'That was no ladle, that was my knife.'"

Shirley laughed appreciatively. Sandy giggled. I watched. Shirley's kids didn't know what was going on. "You get it, don't you?" she said. "That was no lady, that was my wife." Her kids bobbed their heads in unison.

"Is he always this quiet?"

"He's just shy."

I gave my father a dirty look, but he refused to acknowledge it. "Lettuce now praise famous vegetables," he said. "Don't that beet all? I hope they raise my celery. . . ."

Shirley laughed. "Get it? Celery, Salary."

"Turnip your collar. . . ."

"Turn up."

I watched Clyde circle the room. He stopped at the drapes. He lifted his leg.

Shirley screamed. I smirked.

"He's just taking a leek," I said. "Get it?"

Shirley didn't laugh. "I don't think it's appropriate to joke about a thing like that," she said.

She took Clyde by his choke collar and yanked hard. "Sidney," she said. "You said this dog is housebroken."

"He is," I said. "In our house."

"This is *my* house."

"He's not living at your house."

"Haven't you told them, Sidney?"

"I've been waiting for the right moment," he said. He looked at me sheepishly. "I've got a big surprise for you. Shirley and I are getting married next month. The day after your birthday."

"It's our gift to you," Shirley said.

"We'll be one big, happy family," my father said.

Family? We were a family. Me and Sandy and Clyde and my father. And my uncles. Would this big happy family include Uncle Leo's squirrels? I figured Uncle Danny and Uncle Harry would scare Shirley out of her sensible shoes. I knew her kids wouldn't last a minute in one of Uncle Arthur's newspaper tunnels.

Shirley addressed Sandy and me. "I know you children have been through quite a time, so you don't have to call me Mom yet. Shirley will do for now."

I looked at Sandy, who seemed a little dazed. "Where are we going to live?" she asked.

"We'll move here next month," said my father. "Our house just isn't big enough."

"But what about my friends?" Sandy said.

"You can see them whenever you want. We're less than an hour away."

Then it was over. Only my father talked on the way home.

"Shirley's more interesting than you probably think," he said. "Her brother is one of the world's ten best pianists."

Back in my room, I packed some clothes, the dog bowl and all twelve of my lucky bucks. Clyde and I went out to the sweet gum tree and sat down to think. I could run away and not come back until my father agreed to call off the wedding, but he'd probably just marry someone else. Maybe worse. I continued to ponder my options until just before dinner time, and found none that were acceptable. Then I remembered the advice Uncle Danny gave me way back when I was eight: "Don't play the game."

"Don't play the game," I said to Clyde.

He gave me his OK look.

I went back to my room and gathered the cherry bombs Ash had left the day he tried to blast Clyde. I took down the planets and rockets whirring just below the ceiling—my father's universe—and lugged them out to the driveway and blew them up, one by one.

Chapter 10

Ashes to Ashes

I never did call Shirley Mom. I never called her Shirley, either. I never called her anything, except once when, bursting with teenage righteousness, I called her a shit.

A week after I met her, Shirley came to our house. She marched through the rooms taking stock of our furniture like a constable at a sheriff's sale. My father followed, acquiescent, happy to abdicate his authority to her.

"This chair is all right. . . . That lamp is no good. . . . This can stay. . . . That has to go. . . . Throw this out. . . . I'll put that in the attic. . . ." I watched this stranger trail her fingers over the artifacts of our lives. The most ordinary trinkets, the everyday dishes in the kitchen cabinets, the glass ashtrays in which my mother had rested her cigarettes, had become precious and evocative since her death. I cringed.

I ran ahead through the living room and the kitchen and the den, the rooms from which my mother's presence was rapidly vanishing. I felt like breaking everything, but fled to the basement instead. When I got to the bottom of the steps, I saw my mother's typewriter in the place it had always been. I rolled in a piece of paper and typed: S-H-I-R-L-E-Y I-S A S-H-I-T.

This was my first piece of writing for an audience. I knew Shirley would find it; she was as thorough as a bank examiner. She kept it for as long as I lived in her house, brandishing the ragged page forth every time we renewed our endless running argument. She was like a prosecuting attorney presenting Exhibit A. For the rest of my adolescence, Shirley and I were locked in silent—or often not-so-silent—warfare.

In Shirley's house, Sandy and I were encumbrances that came with my father, a form of baggage that she—or I—never allowed him to unpack. Shirley firmly believed in family life, but we never became part of her family. She demanded that we share what we had—our possessions, our emotions—but she didn't offer us much in exchange. Not even Clyde was exempt. Shirley decreed him the "family dog."

Clyde slept by my bed in a den full of boxes and cartons. One night soon after we got there, Shirley's oldest son, George, who was a year younger than me, came in the room and led Clyde away.

I headed George off at the door.

"It's my turn to have Clyde," he said.

"Says who?"

"My mother."

"He's my dog."

We both had our hands on Clyde's collar. He tugged. I pulled back. George's face came up to mine. I punched him in the mouth.

He ran to get his mother.

Shirley arrived glaring.

"Clyde is now the family dog," she declared.

"Yeah," I said. "My family's, not yours."

My father stumbled in, his eyebrows set in perplexed diagonals. "What happened?" he asked.

"Your son punched George," Shirley said between sharp little breaths. She was livid. "For no reason."

My father turned to me. "Why'd you beat up George?" he asked.

"Clyde's my dog," I said.

"He didn't beat me up," George said.

My father turned to Shirley.

"It's George's turn to have the dog," she said. "From now on, the children will take turns with the dog. I've already discussed this with you."

"Nobody discussed it with me," I said.

"Don't you think Shirley's kids should have turns, too?" my father asked.

"No."

"Well, if they can't have terns, how about pelicans?"

"Sidney!" said Shirley. "Punching is not allowed in my house."

"I didn't punch him," I said. "I smote him."

"Didn't you see the no smoting sign?" asked my father.

"Sidney!"

"Next time," he said, "don't beat up George, OK?"

"He didn't beat me up," George protested.

"All right, Dad," I said. "I won't beat him up again."

"You didn't beat me up."

"See, Shirley," my father said. "That wasn't so difficult, was it?" He strolled out of the room, the scientist satisfied that resolving dissension in the family was as easy as eliminating distortion in a hi-fi system. Shirley slipped me her icy stare. She led George out and slammed the door behind her.

I lay in bed with my hands laced behind my head, eyes wide open. Clyde and I listened to snatches of Shirley twitting my father: "That wasn't the way to handle it, Sidney. . . . From now on . . . He had no right. . . . From now on . . . In my house . . ."

Shirley was such a tightly clamped spring that she never allowed herself a moment of casual laughter or casual pique. She was always complaining about something. If it wasn't me, it was Clyde or her first husband, Bernie, the doctor she put through medical school. Bernie took off with another woman and moved to Rhode Island. He left Shirley with two sons, a daughter and a fetus in formaldehyde. He'd brought the fetus home from class one day and for some reason, Shirley had never thrown it away.

When Shirley got angry, she sometimes called *me*

Bernie. But mostly she stuck to "you spoiled teen-ager" or just plain "Stephen."

My mother had named me Stephen, but nobody had ever called me that. I was always Steve or Little Stevie. Shirley always called me "Steven." She hissed the S and pronounced the V as though it were the edge of a razor. I came to loathe the name.

In Shirley's house, I felt like a Marine in a bunker besieged by the Vietcong. Her kids peeped out from behind their doors like sappers waiting in ambush. We didn't speak, even at dinner. They ate with a gnashing of teeth that suggested to me a column of advancing troops. These small dental concatenations were accompanied by the rattle of my father's puns and the whine of Shirley's sniping.

A few months after we moved in, Shirley noticed that several boxes of books that had been in a corner of the den were gone. In a moment of extreme boredom—well, more than that—I had combed through them and replaced her volumes on self-improvement with my father's existentialist canon. I consigned Shirley's books to the attic. She confronted me with my heinous misdeed.

"Stephen," she said, "how do you have the right to rearrange books that belong to your father and me, and decide which should be left on the shelves and which should be packed away? The only things in this house that are your property to do entirely what you please with are things that belong to you alone, things which you purchased with your own money."

I listened, my arms folded across my chest. My father came into the room to listen, too.

"Stephen," she said, "if at some time I want your advice on how to arrange my library, or on the relative literary merits of various books, I will ask you. And if you have a criticism of how things are arranged in the house, you are free to express your feelings, vocally. But keep your cotton-pickin' hands off. Stop acting like a spoiled teenager. You are not allowed to change the way my books are stacked."

"Eleanor Roosevelt was stacked," I said coolly.

"How dare you!" said Shirley.

"You don't think her tits were big?"

"Sidney! Are you going to let him get away with that?"

"Of course not," said my father. "Eleanor Roosevelt was a large woman. She had grandmotherly tits."

"Sidney! That word will not be used in my house."

"Which one?" I asked. "Stacked or tits?"

"Sidney, I demand that you punish him."

"For what? For improving our reading setup?"

I was grateful for my father's unexpected support, and took advantage of the moment to leave.

"Remain seated, Stephen!" commanded Shirley.

I kept walking. Shirley shrieked at my back. Then she shrieked at my father, who grabbed one of her prized china cups and hurled it against the wall. He charged out of the house and drove to the library. An hour later he was back. He sat down at the dinner table, a bottle of glue and the pieces of china before him.

My father counted on things to work themselves out. He felt he had done his domestic duty when he found a mother for his two children. He accepted Shirley's three kids as part of the deal, but he never considered the possibility that two plus three wouldn't equal five. And when they didn't, he threw up his hands and walked away.

My relationship with Shirley was as fragile as her china—it shattered from its own brittle tensions. At fourteen, all my conversations with her ended in argument. At fifteen, they all began with argument. By the time I was sixteen, our conversations were all argument. Sandy was more submissive. She retreated to her room, wedging towels under the door to muffle the bickering. She had tried to earn Shirley's acceptance by cooking meals, vacuuming the floors, doing the laundry. Shirley was perfectly willing to have a maid living in her house, but she didn't want another daughter. She had started out with only a limited fund of affection, and now it appeared she was bankrupt.

Even Clyde became displaced. He'd had a free run of our house. Now he was chained up in Shirley's backyard most days. He growled at phantoms and stalked ghosts.

I was insubordinate at home and sardonic outside. I was sixteen and had a crush on a girl named Wendy, a slightly oddball character who pursed her lips in a half-amused, half-abashed smile as if she'd heard an off-color joke she didn't quite get. Wendy really liked me, I think, but I was never quite sure why. I was tall and reedy and as fearfully awkward as any sixteen-year-old, but more mistrustful than most. I couldn't give up my father's offputting word-play or my small war with my stepmother or the long hollowness of my hurt at the loss of my mother. Some kid to have a crush on.

Wendy and I would go to foreign films and make out, and when Marcello Mastroianni walked through the existential gardens with Monica Vitti, Wendy would warm against my shoulder and say something nice. I'd usually abandon existentialism for a wiseguy line from Humphrey Bogart—"I won't play the sap for you"—as noncommittal as my father.

She called one afternoon before dinner.

"Could you come over?" she asked. I could hardly hear her.

"What for?" I said.

"Don't you know my father died this morning?"

"No, but hum a few bars and I'll get it."

Wendy hung up. I actually felt offended that she hadn't humored me. I hemmed and hawed for an hour before I went over. She wouldn't talk to me, and I didn't really have anything to say to her, either. I felt like my father, moored in dead responses. I felt hateful.

One night when I was seventeen, Ash appeared at the house. It was cool and wet; a sort of misty rain hovered in the air. My father answered the door.

"Who are you?" I heard him ask.

"I sold Charles Manson the map of the stars' homes. I'm making one of this neighborhood. Would you like to be on it?"

I hardly recognized Ash. It had been two years since I'd seen him. Trimmed with plebelike precision, his hair rose stiff as quills. His eyes were swollen and set deep in their sockets. The only hint of insolence was his bare feet. He'd been kicked out of junior high soon after our afternoon at the supermarket and shipped to a military academy modeled along the lines of Holden Caulfield's Pencey Prep: It was designed to mold rich kids into splendid, clear-thinking young men.

"What have you been up to?" I asked.

"Getting laid. Shooting speed. Growing a goatee."

I took Ash upstairs to see Bernie's fetus. I knew the grotesque figure submerged in formaldehyde would captivate him. I handed Ash the jar. He turned it and turned it slowly in his hands.

"Ash?" I said. He looked weird.

He didn't answer. Holding the jar to his chest, he hurried downstairs and out the door. I couldn't stop him, but I knew Shirley would be coming after me with a flamethrower if she realized the fetus was missing.

Ash climbed into his convertible. I got in, too. He put the jar on the dash like a plastic Madonna.

"This poor little bastard never got born, did he?" Ash said. "He was lucky, wasn't he? Never got to live. Never got to think he'd want to die. And now

he floats here forever. . . ." A smile flashed across
his face that was broad and fishy and diabolical.
". . . Unless I throw this bottle into the street and
smash it."

"Don't, Ash," I pleaded. "My stepmother's going
to kill me as it is."

Laughing derisively, Ash revved the engine and
jammed the car through the gears. We peeled off,
the motor whining. I smelled burning rubber. We
skidded around narrow suburban curves, screaming
up on a motor scooter and muscled it off the road.
When we got to a railroad crossing, Ash hit the
brakes. He seized the jar and tossed it at me. I was
just able to catch it and keep it from bouncing out
of the car.

He pulled up into the middle of the tracks. I
could hear a train.

"Watch this," Ash said. He had one foot on the
accelerator, the other on the steering wheel.

He revved the engine again. "You're fucking
nuts," I screamed, scrambling out the door, clutching the jar like a football. The train bore down. Ash
stayed put.

"Get out! Get out!" I yelled; I was sure he was
going to die. I was sure he wanted to.

Just as the train reached the crossing, Ash
slammed into first. The car squealed off the tracks
an instant ahead of the train. He whooped defi-
antly, yelling "Fuck you, you scared little shit!" and
roared away.

I walked home, a mile, afraid and angry. Ash had

almost killed me. He'd always been crazy, but now he was terrifying.

A few days later one of the guys from our old junior high called to tell me Ash had shoved the barrel of a mail-order rifle into his mouth and pulled the trigger with his big toe.

I had a vision of Ash's head exploding, his brain spreading over the glass door of the living room where he had been sitting. I imagined him lying dead, the minutes ticking away until he was found. This image returned at odd and unpredictable moments. Even to this day. I imagine the gun and Ash's bare feet and I hear the bang and I wish he were alive.

Chapter 11

Did Someone Call Me Schnorrer?

Uncle Harry came along just in time to be the unstrung hero I needed. New York State was clearing out its asylums in the late 1960s. The nuts, benign and otherwise, were dumped out onto the streets, where they were left to proselytize on behalf of their alternative universes. Uncle Harry was one of the gentler ones. His message was: Don't just avoid reality, ignore it.

I had never met him, and wouldn't until I was out of college and on my own. I knew him largely by the letters he'd been sending me since my Bar Mitzvah. His prose read like the notes of an eccentric stockbroker: *"Page a, Series 1967 . . . This is History! . . . Inform me via correspondence when you receive it . . . also condition of item you verify."* Sometimes it was a little too cryptic. One letter read, in its entirety: *"Cancan dancers are always hungry."* Another one: *"Happy Pal's Day."* A third: *Happy Arabian New Year."*

Uncle Harry never sent me a card for my birthday, though he invariably let me know when his was coming up. But we often exchanged gifts. He liked to trade "evens evens." When I was in the eleventh grade I mailed him a can of pipe tobacco, and he sent me an all-day sucker and a pack of Parliaments. "The lollipop was great," I wrote back, "but the white sticks tasted awful."

A certified letter arrived later that week. "You eat the candy or suck on it," Uncle Harry instructed. "However, the Parliament cigarettes you smoke in at your mouth between your lips by puffing long breaths, first in . . . then out!"

He wrote in a cramped hand that tended to droop toward the right side of the page, a rapid, ragged scrawl that people who think faster than they write can develop. He sealed his letters inside well-taped double envelopes on which he scratched explicit instructions for the postman. He spelled out what to do if it proved undeliverable in eleven, fourteen or seventeen days, and where, amid the semi-indecipherable scribbling, the stamp was hidden. And he always stuck on a return-address label that read:

> HARRY LIDZ
> PRESIDENT OF ATHLETICS
> RETIRED UNDEFEATED

In that rich fantasy land where every sports fan is a champion, Uncle Harry was the world's greatest boxer. He'd fought in boxing clubs around Washington Heights in the late twenties, but he hadn't actually been in the ring since 1931. Nevertheless in the arenas of his mind, he won fight after fight. His imaginary career reached its pinnacle when he retired as the undefeated champion of nine amateur divisions from featherweight to light heavyweight. "There was nobody left to fight me," he explained.

In 1957, when Uncle Harry was forty-four, he drew a self-portrait of himself in boxing gear and chronicled his domination of amateur boxing along the margins. He pictured himself as an Egyptian prince, a featherweight standing tall and two-dimensional, his left arm jabbing and his right arm cocked. Uncle Harry used crayons from a sixty-four-pack Crayola box. He gave himself white trunks and plum-colored gloves. Across the bottom of the drawing he wrote: "World's undefeated and retired Y and AAU Boxing Champion, 1930 & 1931 and earlier." He sent it to me for my sixteenth birthday, and I hung it on my bedroom wall. Whenever I moved, the first thing I did was hang Uncle Harry's portrait on the wall. His picture hangs in my bedroom now. It reminds me not to get too attached to the real world.

Uncle Harry's opponents had strange nicknames, but their given names were even stranger. In one letter he writes: "On March 28, 1932, I was challenged by Thratcher Muggs Charlemaine Fitzsimmons, alias Otto Ott, alias King Willie of Germany, alias Apocalypse Death. I stopped him in the second round with three solid rights. The referee made me watch the count."

"Why did he stop the fight?" I wrote back.

The reply arrived in one of Uncle Harry's double-sealed envelopes, marked Special Delivery: "I broke his head."

I always wondered how much of this Uncle Harry really believed. So one day I wrote him and asked, straight out. Uncle Harry sensed an emergency. A registered letter with a presidential return label showed up three days later: "It is not permitted to defame me. My winnings are actual, not fantasy. Praised be the Gods and Goddesses! I am for Liberty for everyone, also all. Slander and infamy are not civilized, nor lawful, either. I am Harry Lidz, authentic champion."

My father told me Uncle Harry was a good amateur, but he was never really a contender. In fact, he never fought for anything after he was knocked out in the first minute of the first round of his only Golden Gloves bout. It must have been some punch, because from that time on Uncle Harry thought of himself as world champion.

Uncle Harry had been a bit of a hero in real life. During the thirties all the brothers were Reds—of varying hues from pink to crimson. Uncle Harry was the most committed. While Uncle Arthur led the blind vendor around Hoboken, Uncle Danny davened in shul, Uncle Leo dreamed of Raskolnikov and my father studied calculus, Uncle Harry volunteered for the Abraham Lincoln Brigade in the Spanish Civil War. He was a courier with the Loyalist forces around Valencia and Badajoz. He became famous for his ability to sneak in and out of the trenches while under fire. My father said Uncle Harry was called *La Cucaracha*, the cockroach—a nom de guerre Uncle Harry disavowed. "I am not a cockroach," he insisted, "nor an insect."

Looking back now, I suppose there came a moment when I adopted Uncle Harry's style of evasion, which was to ignore reality if it became too painful. This worked for me when we moved in with Shirley: The most effective way to irritate her was to ignore her. It came to me sometime during my sixteenth year that my uncles' goofy, misdirectional approach to life was the direct opposite of Shirley's corseted suburbanism.

I could date my uncle-ization from the day I became Franz, the name Uncle Harry called me in all his letters. I was taking a quiz in a geometry class and my mind wandered to Uncle Harry in the ring, dancing with shoulders forward, eyes squinched, dispatching opponents with sudden, whamming fists. He reminded me of Popeye. The Sailor Man's anthem ran through my head

> I'm one tough Gazookus
> Which hates all Palookas
> Wot ain't on the up and square
> I biffs 'em and buffs 'em
> And always outroughs 'em
> An' none of 'em gets nowhere.

The school bell rang. With a small flourish, I found myself signing Franz Lidz to the test sheet before I stuck it under my teacher's nose. He glanced at the signature.

"Were you composing something, Mr. Lidzt?" he joked.

"Myself," I said.

Shirley never accepted Franz. When my friends called and asked for Franz, Shirley demanded, "Do you want Stephen?" She sent me Hannukah cards addressed to Stephen. She brought my seventeenth-birthday cake inscribed "Happy Birthday, Stephen" to the dinner table.

"My name is Franz" I said deliberately, trying to summon up the same cool indignation Uncle Harry had when his boxing prowess was challenged.

"Stephen," Shirley said. She pronounced the

name with heavy finality, like a mason placing the last stone in a wall.

"Whether you like it or not," she said, "*I* am the one who bought your birthday cake. *I* am the one who bought the card. *I* signed the check inside. *I* am the one who fills out forms and letters requesting college loans for you. You should be thankful to me, not your father. Do I make myself clear?"

The whole family was at the table, my father, Sandy and Shirley's three children. My father and Sandy looked stunned. The others all sat up, exceedingly erect like trained dogs awaiting their cue.

"Now just a minute," I said, turning on a fake congeniality. My demeanor was open, expansive, scornful—the new me: the unflappable Franz Lidz. "Let me get this straight: Am I the spoiled teenager or the wicked stepmother? I always forget."

"That's it, Stephen! I've had it with you, I really have. Punish him, Sidney."

"What for?" my father asked.

"For not answering my question."

"You didn't answer his."

"Sidney! You're always taking his side. He's your son, but I'm the one you married and come home to. You should support me."

I got up and began to dance Uncle Danny's jig.

"Remain seated, Stephen!"

I remained jigging.

"All right, I'll punish you myself." For the first time, she raised her hand to slap me. I laughed, knowing I'd won a small, mean victory. I danced away. She gave chase. Everyone—her kids, Sandy, my father—watched us circle the dinner table. After the second lap I stopped and turned to face her like Uncle Harry in the ring. Then I laughed again, Uncle Leo's maniacal laugh, his bleating woodpecker laugh.

Shirley opened her mouth, but her words tumbled out in a flustered babble. She looked around the table and saw that even her own children looked as if they wanted to be somewhere else. Shirley stared, pulled herself up straight and marched out of the room.

I felt a surge of satisfaction.

Call me Franz.

Chapter 12

I Am Cold, Warm, Frozen

That was my last birthday cake that had Stephen written on it. For almost a year until I went away to college, Shirley and I treated each other with a kind of barbed disdain. My father was an ineffectual mediator. He didn't want to offend either of us. When I left home for NYU I felt like an escapee from a prison camp.

I was in my second semester when my father called me at my dormitory. He asked me to meet him at the Museum of Natural History. "We'll get to talk a little, Franz," he said. He didn't mind calling me Franz. He liked the pun in it.

In the dim light of the Akeley Hall of African Mammals, my father and I sat sipping sundowners at the portable bar that was set out every afternoon. Eight enormous East African elephants loomed over us, forever ready to stampede. Behind them hartebeest, brindled gnu and Grant's gazelles grazed near a copse of umbrella acacia.

Stuffed and mounted, frozen in their trumpeting charge, the pachyderms seemed to be headed for

Central Park. As a kid I had stood in the semidarkness and marveled at the lead bull, imagining his fearful rumble. In the dioramas encircling this colossal centerpiece, the tawny veldt of Africa stretched magically on forever.

My father often asked me to meet him at the museum. He loved it as much as I did. (He had, in fact, designed the mechanism for the museum's first talking exhibit: Touch a button and from a little metal grill a machinelike voice told you about the Serengeti Plain.) Since I'd left for college, he and I had maintained a sort of clandestine correspondence. I wrote him at his office every week, passing along the impassioned revelations of an eighteen-year-old: "We live in a purgatory named civilization in which people in their mechanized lifestyles oscillate from dull home to dull job amid monumental gravestones of steel and brick that remind the feeling few that this is Man's present glory, Man's present heroism, Man's manmade God."

He edited out any jabs at Shirley, Xeroxed the rest of my adolescent insights and brought the letters home. Shirley asked why I sent photocopies. He said I was "avant-gardening." The pruning is something he kept up for years.

His own letters to me began coherently enough, but invariably digressed into nonsensical generalizations, unfinished sentences and long-winded maunderings about the ambiguity of life. Some were as arcane and indecipherable as the writings of the densest French semiotician. Others resembled Uncle Harry's, the main difference being where the tape was affixed. My father always taped a twenty-dollar bill inside, which, of course, he kept secret from Shirley.

Occasionally something meaningful would slip out: "Shirley has been trying to enforce her 'discipline' on Sandy. I go along when it's reasonable, but Saturday night was just too much. It's just the way Shirley expresses herself, and the way Sandy answers that leads to war. Sandy leaves the letters you send her around—possibly unintentionally. It would be easiest for everybody if you left out the little digs about Shirley—after all, you must realize that I do intend spending the rest of my natural life or so with her. I only broke one china cup, but I'd prefer breaking nothing."

His passive appeasement provoked me. I was finally on my own, out of the house, free of Shirley. Independent. Rebellion pulsed through the campus. The Cambodian invasion had refueled student protest. We were on strike. Classes had been called off. Militants occupied the student computer center. I wanted to shake my father up. I wanted to kidnap him. I wanted to liberate him from Shirley.

At the museum, my father looked like he was going to march into one of the dioramas. He wore khaki shorts, white knee socks and sturdy walking shoes. Take off his string tie and he could have been Francis Macomber. I figured I'd end his short happy life with a shot between the eyes.

"So how's life in hell?" I asked.

He leaned into the table like a rower about to take a particularly long stroke. "The answer is—I was a slave in Egypt."

"So how's life in hell?"

"How far down the evolutionary path do you want me to go?"

"So how's—"

"To the memory of the primal cell?"

"—life in—"

"How about the memory of pure energy before it became primordial hydrogen?"

"—hell?"

As he talked, his body rose and rocked in a little dance to the music of his words. He set their tempo with two fingers of his right hand, like an overly energetic bandleader. "Spinoza said, 'We are in many ways driven about by external causes, and like the waves of the sea driven by contending winds, we are swayed hither and thither, unconscious of the issue of our destiny.' Freedom and rationality come only through understanding: To be free you must know the causes and internalize them."

"So . . . how's . . . life . . . in . . . hell?" If I let my father go on talking about Spinoza, his monologue would never stop.

He swirled his sundowner. I could see he was starting to get annoyed. But he tried another exhortation. "Most shit-headed engineers think it's no business of theirs to see what the electronic toys they design do to the world. I think a new set of values must be established for modern man. Man's essence, wrote Sartre, is his existence. What right does technology—through its tool, the technologist—have to show the promise of how we can have abundance for all, but instead, by its deeds, threaten that . . ."

I shouted. "SO HOW'S LIFE IN HELL?"

He winced. He looked across the table to the bartender and the waiter. Nobody seemed ready to come over and throw us out. "Everything's about the same," he said in a careful, measured tone, "but it's bound to improve sometime."

"You really think so?"

He stood up and grasped the edge of the table. "Look, rage only nourishes rage. You don't always have to say what's on your mind."

"You don't?"

"Don't embarrass Shirley by coming out with the fact that I said at some time that she was unreasonable—or worse."

"Why not?"

"Shirley does these things and I criticize her for them."

"I never heard you criticize her."

"Shirley's behavior can be explained in all sorts of psychological manners, but it boils down to her need as an ambitious, able and intelligent being to *be* something in the outside world, to achieve dignity and recognition."

"That's probably true, but she picks a hell of a way to do it."

"I know her authoritarianism toward you and Sandy is often intolerable. I know I have a responsibility and desire to bolster your self-image. Just remember: I'm the guy getting squeezed in the middle.

"In the theoretical sense, I don't need any bullshit dignity and respect—I have enough self-confidence. Yet I need to breast a few things with Shirley now and then as a moral-slash-morale exercise."

I grunted in disbelief.

"Shirley has asked why I accept your letters," he said. "She says if I really respected her, I'd return them marked 'wrong address,' and insist you write to the house. I explained that you find it difficult writing to a place where you can't expect sympathetic acceptance and love, and I only broke one glass—a twenty-seven-year-old heirloom—in the course of the explanation."

"That's putting her in her place!"

My sarcasm derailed the conversation. He yanked on his tie as if it were a ripcord. I stepped away from the table, turned toward the rhinoceros exhibit. The great, blundering beast was frozen in a pose of rage. Suddenly, my father grabbed me from behind in a headlock.

I jerked myself free. "What are you doing!"

"Life's a game, Franz," he said with a weary fatalism. "Before you get involved, first find out whether you're a bat or a ball. You might avoid a walloping."

I felt sorry for him, trotting out this ridiculous wordplay, and came to his rescue: "How do you know what's fair and foul?"

"Know how?"

"No, how?"

"Knowhow."

I'd let him get away once again.

He finally told me why he'd wanted to meet me. Uncle Danny had called him in a panic. The superintendent of their building threatened eviction if Uncle Arthur didn't move out his papers from their pack-rat apartment. The super was afraid the place would burn down. Uncle Arthur adamantly refused. So my father volunteered to help out. He'd volunteered me, too. We had to go. Right then.

I *was* worried about my uncles. A month earlier Danny had called me from a pay phone.

"Meet me and Arthur at Katz's in an hour," he said. He spoke with the terrible urgency of a rabbi who needs one more body for a minyan.

"Is anything wrong?"

"Is anything right?"

They were already sitting down in the old Houston Street cafeteria when I arrived.

"Order anything you want," said Uncle Danny.

"Under a dollar," said Uncle Arthur.

Uncle Danny got a burned hot dog, which he wouldn't eat, and black coffee, which he wouldn't drink. Uncle Arthur loaded up his tray with free sauerkraut.

"I'm quitting my job," Uncle Danny announced.

"What do you mean you're quitting?" I said. "You've had it twelve years."

"They found out where I live."

"They finally found out your street address?"

"No, the borough. They know I live in the Bronx."

"So what do you want me to do."

"Tell them I quit."

"What are you going to do for money?"

"Arthur's still working at *his* messenger job."

So I phoned Uncle Danny's office and had his final paycheck forwarded to a postal box in the Bronx. I hadn't heard from my uncles since.

Their street had the same sour, slightly derelict look I remembered from my last visit ten years before. Uncle Arthur was waiting on the sidewalk when we pulled up. He stood beneath the towering trees that kept his tenement in perpetual shadow. He wore a rust-colored overcoat, chino trousers rolled to the high-water mark, a wide tartan blazer denoting an unknown clan and several multicolored floral shirts. The corners of his hair stuck out like magpie wings. Behind him, Uncle Danny was a-sputter with agitation. He alternately hunched over like Rufus T. Firefly in *Duck Soup* and reared back like the Lone Ranger atop Silver. He had a vaguely Anglo-Irish look: tweed jacket with matching tam, white Oxford shirt and an untamed gray mustache. On his feet were leather moccasins with little beaded birds sewn on the toes.

The apartment was even more run-down than I recalled. Glass was broken out of one of the windows. The wind rustled through, stirring scraps of paper and rattling an old street sign. The foyer reeked of oils and emulsions. Plaster had fallen from the ceiling, crushed open a crate of patent medicines and broken the bottles.

Uncle Arthur conducted us through the newspaper catacombs, the curator of his own collection of precious curiosa. He had spruced up the entrance with plastic bouquets, a fake rubber plant and an eleven-branch electric candelabra, one bulb missing and one burned out.

My father eyed the scene clinically. "Freud said hoarding is a fastidious compulsion rooted in severely repressive early toilet training," he said.

"And for that they put his name on museum walls!" said Uncle Danny, laughing ironically.

I watched amused as my father carried out the junk as compulsively as Uncle Arthur had collected it. He tracked through the jungle of junk in his safari clothes, a census-taker of salvage, adding, sorting, bundling. He counted out two hundred and seventy-five tins of sardines, one hundred and twenty-four trusses, one hundred and two cans of black shoe polish, eighty-eight ice cube trays, one hundred and nine doorknobs, two hundred and thirty-five teacup handles, two hundred and seventeen unopened jars of instant coffee.

"Why all the coffee?" he asked.

"I had coupons," Uncle Arthur replied.

"Why so much?"

"We might get snowed in."

"You expecting another Ice Age?"

Uncle Arthur didn't bother answering. He was pointing out can openers. "A hundred and thirty-three!" he said. "Good ones! Clean ones!"

My father began to sieve through several small Everests of shoelaces.

"Don't touch those piles, Sidney," said Uncle Arthur sharply.

"Why not?" demanded my father.

"They're in order."

"You've actually sorted them?"

"It's hell of a job. Sometimes they have no tips and six different knots to untangle. And that's not even the hardest part of collecting them."

"What is?" I asked.

"Waiting for runners to jump out of their shoes."

My father had reached the end of the line. He cupped his hands over his ears. "Give it up, Arthur," he said.

"Never, Sidney. I see new laces every day. Millions of laces, millions of shoes. Still got feet in them, but they'll wear out. I'll get the laces. I got time."

"Uncle Danny," I said, "what do you think of Uncle Arthur's collection?"

"I don't. Thinking is dangerous. Look at Sidney."

But my father was already hauling bundles down

to the basement incinerator. Meanwhile, Uncle Arthur was hauling them to one of the bedrooms. His eyes looked pained.

"Give me a hand, Franz," my father said.

"I don't really want to."

"Why?"

"Uncle Arthur's spent years collecting these things."

"He doesn't collect, he accumulates."

"What's the difference?"

He snatched up a cruddy truss. "Does this look like a Sèvres vase to you?"

"To Uncle Arthur it does."

"Don't get sentimental. It's a health hazard. It's trash! It's crap!"

"But it's his trash and his crap."

My father eyed me narrowly. Uncle Danny stepped in, suddenly the peacemaker. He took my arm and led me to a flap of sheet metal on which he had set out tea, cookies and assorted Lidziana. A heart-shaped wedding portrait of my grandparents hung on the wall over the sink.

"A wonderful woman, your grandmother," said Uncle Danny. "Mama told me years ago, she told me, 'Your father was born in the Polish town of Lidzbark, which is where we got our name.'"

Thank God, I thought, Simon took Lidz instead of Bark.

"Papa spoke in tongues, Franzie, almost as soon as he could talk: Yiddish, Polish, English, German, Greek, Syrian, Arabic. He wasn't twenty before he was traveling around Europe teaching languages. The ones he knew best, nobody else even remembered: Phoenician, Punic, Assyrian."

"Your grandfather's bent was more cryptography than conversation," my father said from beneath an arch of papers. He was having fun throwing out Uncle Arthur's junk. He sang the Rag Man song while he worked:

> Any rags?
> Any rags?
> Any bags, any bones any bottles today?
> It's the same old story in the same old way.

He sounded like a Rag Man. His singing voice was hoarse and scratchy, having never fully recovered from that polyp operation years ago.

"Papa heard they needed language teachers in America," said Uncle Danny. "He came in 1889."

My father came through with more papers.

"Unfortunately," he said, "not too many people on the Lower East Side wanted to learn Punic, so your grandfather went to work in the needle trades, in a sweatshop, like every other immigrant Jew in New York."

"He taught Mama English," Uncle Danny admonished my father. "And all the rest of the Borowitzes."

Spread out before me on the sheet metal, the family memorabilia had the oddly disconnected quality of pages torn at random from a diary. But the grand array was dazzling: a crest someone had drawn for the hearty eaters of the Borowitz clan—a cup of steaming coffee and a pair of forked frankfurters crossed over a plate of beans; the rhinestone-studded turban Simon had worn when he taught my grandmother English—he'd appeared before her like some Byzantine rabbi come to instruct the Turk; the handwritten Yiddish-English phrasebook he had used to teach her. Thumbing through its musty pages, I imagined Simon and Fannie talking to each other in phrasebook singsong:

Simon: "What sort of weather is it?"

Fannie: "It is cold, hot, fine, bad."

Simon: "How do you feel?"

Fannie: "I am cold, warm, frozen."

I scoured the book for the racy parts, but as far as I could tell, there wasn't even a phrase for holding hands.

Uncle Danny took his cap off. His hair was plastered to his head. He stirred his tea. He gestured toward the cookies: Take more.

My father, still working, continued to serenade us with the Rag Man song:

> Any hats?
> Any spats?
> Any cats? Any rats? Any garbage today?
> Just wait a minute, I'm coming your way.

In the wedding portrait over the sink, Fannie was demure in a high lace collar, a dress heavily laden

with ivory taffeta, and, in her hair, a sprig of laven-
der: the very image of a respectable bourgeois
bride. Simon, her well-barbered groom, wore a stiff
collar, black and white bowtie, and, on his
lapel, a lush carnation. But a cacophony of internal
disharmonies resounded in his face: an imposing
patriarchal mustache, a discomfited scholar's scowl
around the eyes gave way to the sudden, unsettling
smile of a con man. Simon projected supreme confidence, Fannie, a little hesitation. She didn't know
yet she should have been a whole lot more hesitant.

"Papa never told her," Uncle Danny said.

"Told her what?"

"About his other wife back in Poland. Mama had
me and Leo before she found out."

The story he told me came out like one of the
Tales of the Fathers. Fannie insisted she and Simon
sleep head to toe, in a sort of rabbinic remedy for
bigamy. After six years of inverted and celibate
slumber, word came from Poland that the other
wife was dead.

"Whereupon my Uncle Nathan drove her and my
father to Jersey City," said Uncle Danny. "Whereupon the marriage was renewed."

Whereupon Fanny realigned her pillow with Simon's.

And whereupon Harry, Arthur and my father
came in rapid succession.

"Franz! Dan! Come quick!" said my father. He
had unearthed his parents' mattress. The bedding
was torn and stained. A cigar box protruded from

the straw stuffing. Inside were four wood plugs, one paper clip and a cracker tin filled with spent moth balls.

Uncle Danny continued to grope around in the straw and extracted a handful of discolored wooden checkers; the sight of them sparked one of his tirades. "Checkers killed Papa! Day and night it was checkers, checkers, checkers. Never did get a rematch with Richard Jordan. Hit by a trolley, Jordan was. In Edinburgh. Dragged forty feet. Never came out of the coma, they said. Served him right, the SOB. Over and over Papa replayed his moves. Over and over and over. Stayed down in the basement of the shrinking company. Couldn't get him away from the board. Mama found him. Slumped over. Dead."

"Didn't you once tell me he'd been assassinated?"

"Assassinated? That's putting it mildly! You know what was imbedded in his forehead? That's right, a checker!"

It was dark outside when Uncle Danny finally gave up talking. My father, too, surrendered. In eight hours, he'd hardly made a dent in the wall of detritus.

"I'm sorry, Arthur," he said. "We had to start some time. The Frick Museum it ain't, but you've got some good junk. Collecting can have a purpose. People in Transylvania collect garlic to string over their doors."   ·

As usual, my father offered an esoteric fact as consolation: "It keeps out evil spirits."

"What's the matter?" Uncle Arthur said. "Don't they have screens?"

He handed me a bag crammed with the usual assortment of his whimsical gifts: grimy balls, empty cigarette packs and seventh-hand comic books, the same stuff I treasured when I was eight. All this rooting around left me with the small, sad feeling that we were throwing out the past.

I fished out an old phonograph record.

"Look, Dad! A seventy-nine."

"What do you mean? Records only come in thirty-three, forty-five and seventy-eight."

"This one's a seventy-nine," I said. "It's faster."

Chapter 13

Repealing the Law
of Gravity

September 8, 1971

Dear Franz,

The halvah you sent me was great. I had to eat it
at work, though. If I took it home, I'd have to ex-
plain why you sent it to my office, and if I reached
a position of honesty at the house, I would have to
admit it was my own fault because if I write from
work to be able to say a few extra personal things I
imply a desire for some privacy between us. And
that is true, but if you could send an occasional to-
ken note home, it would be even nicer.

Love, Dad

I had transferred to a small, progressive liberal arts
school, where I was unencumbered by tests and
term papers and grades. I did pretty much what I
wanted. And I wanted to become an actor.

Acting came naturally to me. My father and his
brothers always seemed to be performing one role
or another in a long series of absurd domestic dra-
mas. They never gave up the acts they had created

for themselves long ago. I just started playing my part, too.

I auditioned conceptually for the tragic role of Othello, dressing as a house painter, in coveralls and a spattered cap. The director was nonplussed.

"I wanted to play Othello not as a noble Moor," I explained, "but as Benjamin Moore."

I never stopped playing some kind of role, mostly Merrie Melodies. Girlfriends miscast me. An ethereal bunch, they saw me as the romantic lead, and I wanted to do comic relief. The plots of my love affairs followed conventional arcs: mutual discovery of endearing foibles, mutual discovery of annoying foibles, then the big breakup.

I played everyone but me, whoever that was, holding myself in with a reserve that no one could breach. If I got too close to revealing any feelings, I'd interrupt myself in mid-thought and stammer to a stop. Talking in conundrums, hiding behind equivocation, I made myself as untouchable as my father.

I found a certain direction when I got a job driving a bus. Every afternoon I steered a minivan through the same suburban streets and ended up in the same suburban mall. The dull ritual was comforting. My bus was often empty: In this new town everybody had a car. I drove alone and liked it. There was no need to perform because I was totally anonymous.

One day a girl got on outside the community playhouse, which may be inevitable in this kind of tale. Maggie was a high school senior with clear, dark eyes and an appealing tangle of black hair. She swung onto the bus with an easy grace. I'd been reeling off lines to myself from *The Bald Soprano*: "I prefer a bird in the bush to a sparrow in a barrow . . . The car goes very fast, but the cook beats batter better."

"What are you talking about?" Maggie said.

"Rather a steak in a chalet than gristle in a castle."

"Is that your idea of a pickup line?"

"It's Ionesco."

"It's corny."

"Corny!"

I could tell immediately that she was my kind of girl: smart, nervy and critically post-modern. All she lacked was twenty-five cents.

I let her ride for nothing.

Maggie took the bus every day after that. She was someone with whom I didn't have to act, with whom I didn't have to make a pun out of every second word, with whom I could talk without forming cryptograms. I found myself doing corny things like buying her roses.

One day we drove to New York. I wanted Maggie to meet my uncles. "You'll like them," I said. "They're like e.e. cummings poems. Uncle Arthur lacks punctuation and Uncle Danny's a little unjustified around the edges."

We were lost on the Bowery when the taxi came through the red light. Maggie screamed: "Franz!"

The taxi smashed into the door on her side. My Volkswagen rolled over and then over again. Maggie and I swirled around like clothes in a washer. We turned over one more time. The windshield shattered. Glass splintered around us. The VW stopped upside down. Something crushed me. Everything was splashed with blood: me, Maggie, the car. Maggie was limp in my lap.

I squeezed out through the window, pulling Maggie out behind me. I was afraid the glass was cutting her body. I stood up in the street holding her in my arms and believing she was dead. I wanted to howl, like Uncle Leo in the nuthouse.

Maggie stirred in my arms. She was alive. She looked up with an enormous grin, a dizzying grin.

"I told you," she said woozily.

"Told me?"

"I told you we should have taken the Lincoln Tunnel."

March 3, 1976

Dear Franz,

I've gradually shifted things over so that I am relatively disengaged from the house and the people in it. This is the season I take judo classes and sailing lessons. It is both more than and less than a sublimation of the sexual urge—it is more a shifting of the emphasis in my life from home and hearth to—at present—trivial outside physical exercises. To the extent that they demand my concentration, they liberate me from constant awareness of home relationships.

Love, Dad

My father, Shirley and her kids had moved to Lexington, Massachusetts. He'd taken a new job. Sandy refused to go with them. She finished high school living at a neighbor's house, Clyde went, but he became fatally irascible. Shirley had him put to sleep.

My father wrote that they moved partly so he could have a house Shirley couldn't claim was hers. In letter after letter he insisted she was improving. He wrote that he encouraged her to take night classes, that he enlisted her help in protesting the crèche on the Lexington battle green. But I could never see a change for the better. Whenever I visited, I saw them arguing. Doors slammed, cups shattered. I'd take the next train out.

After one Thanksgiving visit, Shirley banned Maggie and me from the house. She said I hadn't thanked her for allowing the two of us over. Still, my father wanted me there for Passover the following April. Passover was his only concession to Judaism; it was the only Jewish holiday we'd celebrated with my mother.

"I've discussed the problem with Shirley's sons," he wrote me. "They agree that I should have the right to invite my own children to my own home irrespective of any problems you have with Shirley."

I agreed to come only after he told me Uncle Danny and Uncle Arthur would be there. They had moved to Brooklyn after Uncle Danny was robbed and stabbed in the vestibule of their apartment. "The thought crosses my mind," wrote my father, "that after Dan was held up he might have felt he'd earned the right to castigate his 'oppressor,' and had injury added to insult." Uncle Harry wasn't coming. In those days, he wouldn't leave Buffalo. He only sent photographs, occasionally of himself, but more often of his boxing gear, the meager furniture of his room, the clothes laid out on his bed.

Shirley put up with Uncle Arthur, but she didn't suffer Uncle Danny gladly. She thought he was too unaccountable, too uncompromising, too unpredictable.

Uncle Danny had his own suspicions. He smelled a Passover plot. "Should we go?" he wrote me. "Please send your answer *special delivery!*" We *must* know before we talk to Shirley and Sidney on Sunday! DESTROY THIS LETTER!"

I wrote Uncle Danny I'd see him and Uncle Arthur in Lexington. They asked my father to meet them at the train station in midafternoon. My father and I went, but I wasn't surprised when my uncles failed to show. Uncle Danny called two hours later.

"Where the hell are you?" demanded my father.

"Boston."

"Why didn't you get off where I told you to?"

"The conductor lied. But he couldn't fool us! We stayed put until the final stop."

We drove to Boston to pick them up. Uncle Danny railed against the conductor, the engineer, the passengers—all of whom he thought had connived to keep him from observing Passover. When we finally got back to the house, he was snapping like a high-tension wire, flicking sparks in every direction.

"Can I get you anything, Danny?" Shirley asked.

"A seltzer," he said. "Get me a bottle of seltzer."

She poured some seltzer into a glass and gave it to him.

"I said a *bottle* of seltzer!" Uncle Danny yelled. "I didn't ask you to open it!"

"Stop being abrasive," my father said.

"Shirley's been smoking pot."

"I certainly have not!"

"You think I don't know slurred speech when I hear it? You thought, 'Danny's coming, I need some marijuana.' Am I right or am I right?"

"She doesn't take drugs," said my father.

"And my speech is not slurred," said Shirley.

Uncle Danny clucked his tongue. "Smoking pot in front of the children! You think that's right?"

Before the conversation got totally out of control, my father took out the slides of the twelve-day, eight-city tour of Europe he had just taken with Shirley. A diversion in the living room.

"Here's Shirley in front of the Eiffel Tower. It's nine hundred and eighty-four feet high and weighs seven thousand tons."

Click.

"Here's Shirley in front of the Leaning Tower of Pisa. It was finished six hundred and four years ago and weighs fourteen thousand tons."

Click.

"Here's Shirley in front of the Louvre. The museum was established by decree of the Revolutionary government in seventeen ninety-three."

"How much does it weigh?" asked Uncle Arthur.

My father whipped his head from side to side in mock agony. "The Louvre has two hundred thousand objects on display. By allotting them six seconds apiece, I saw nearly two thousand in four hours."

Uncle Danny clucked again. "That wasn't the Tower of Pisa," he said.

"What are you talking about?" said my father.

"It's a fake, Sidney."

"Stop trying to aggravate me."

"The real one leans the other way."

My father checked the projector. Sure enough, the slide was in backwards. Uncle Danny squealed with delight and did a mad little shuffle without getting up from his place on the sofa.

"Go to hell, Danny!" said my father.

"There, there, Sidney," said Shirley.

"Dorothy Parker said there is no there there," he said.

"I believe it was Gertrude Stein," she said.

"You mean Dorothy Parker said there is no Gertrude Stein?" I said helpfully.

"That's a terrible thing for her to say," said Uncle Danny.

My father looked at me resentfully. Shirley looked at the Louvre. "Franz knows perfectly well what Shirley said," he said.

"Oh, so now Shirley said it," I said.

"Stephen!" said Shirley.

"Shirley!" said Uncle Danny. "Don't try to change your story. Who did say it, you or Dorothy Parker?"

"Dorothy who?" asked Uncle Arthur.

"Her name is unimportant," said my father.

"That's a funny name."

"You can go to hell, too!"

"Doctoring pictures!" said Uncle Danny. "Smoking pot in front of the children! You think that's right?"

I took his arm and escorted him to his seat at the Seder table. Everyone else followed. When he picked up the Haggadah, I watched as my haywire uncle became placid and reverent. He read the Hebrew with fluent ease, a man reciting an old story well learned and well loved. We listened quietly as Uncle Danny led us through the ritual that celebrates the liberation of the Jews from Egypt.

"Ma-nish-ta-naw ha-lai-law ha-zeh mee-kawl he-lay-los." Why is this night different from all other nights?

Because we're all sitting together, I thought. Even Shirley is cordial.

But when Uncle Danny came to the passage in which the hard bondage of mortar and brick was symbolized with bitter herbs and *charoseth,* the mixture of nuts, apples and cinnamon, Uncle Arthur had a hard time. He tried to spread the *charoseth* on the matzoh with his fingers.

"Try a knife, Arthur," said my father.

"Suicide is the coward's way out," Uncle Danny said. He passed me the shankbone, symbolic of sacrifice.

"I guess that rules out ice picks, too."

"You want to see Arthur hacked to death like Trotsky, Sidney? Is that it? Hacked to death with an ice pick?"

"Danny, please!" said Shirley.

"I thought he got whacked with an alpenstock," said my father.

"Sidney, please!"

"What's an alpenstock?" asked Uncle Arthur.

"Ice pick, Sidney, ice pick!" said Uncle Danny, stabbing the air with his fist, his voice shrill, the Haggadah forgotten. "With an ice pick Jackson hacked him."

"Danny, really!" said Shirley. "Not at the dinner table!"

"Dinner table? Who said dinner table? At Trotsky's desk Jackson hacked him. Through his skull, with one terrible swipe. Blood spurting everywhere: through his hair, into his eyes . . ."

"Sidney, make him stop!"

"Who's Jackson?" asked Uncle Arthur.

"I went to the prostitute once," Uncle Danny blurted out, now totally adrift, "but I didn't go back. She manipulated me."

He raised his glass of wine and sang:

> Dare to be a Daniel,
> Dare to be alone,

Dare to be a Daniel,
Dare to make it known.

Uncle Danny hooted and hollered. Shirley poured him a glass of wine. I wondered why. In a moment I knew.

"I've been poisoned!" he screamed. Wine sprayed from his lips in a purple spritz. For once, Uncle Danny's fears were grounded. Shirley wasn't taking any chances. She'd called a doctor to find out how much Valium it would take to sedate Uncle Danny, then spiked his Manischewitz.

"She can't do this to me!" Uncle Danny said.

"She can try," said my father.

"Poisoning relatives! Doctoring pictures! Smoking pot in front of the children! You think that's right?"

This time I walked him to the master bedroom and planted him in an armchair. "An Alka Seltzer," he moaned. "Get me Alka Seltzer." I dropped two tablets in a glass of water. He gulped them down even before they began to fizz.

"Feel like lying down for a while?" I asked.

"I can't lie down. They switch my heart on and off with a pacemaker. Lie down and I black out. Open my eyes and it's six hours later. Mind control. Brainwashing. What else do they call it?"

"Sleep, Uncle Danny. They call it sleep."

"What can I do?" he asked.

Before I could answer, he slapped me hard across the face. I was shocked. My crazy uncle had turned on *me*! "Why'd you change your name?" he demanded. "The S in Stephen stands for Simon, my father."

I thought fast. "But F is for Fannie, your mother."

That pleased him. He abandoned his anger as easily as reality. A sudden, beatific smile appeared on his face. He thanked me and blessed me in Hebrew and laid a big, sloppy kiss on my cheek. Then he did black out.

I caught Uncle Danny in my arms. Lifting him from the chair, I felt his thin bones and his insubstantial flesh. When I laid him gently on the bed, he seemed as ephemeral as his fears, as if his life were draining away. He looked as if he might simply disappear, leaving nothing behind but madness and whispered prayers.

I returned to the Seder table and sat in Uncle Danny's chair. Everyone was gone, but I heard muffled voices quarreling out back in the yard. The meal had ended almost before it began. The dirty plates were still on the table, and in each place the symbolic portion of honey and apple, burnt shankbone, the mortar of *charoseth*, and more than our share of bitter herbs.

Chapter 14

Wheels Spinning, Wheels Singing

Uncle Danny remained abrasive to the very end: He collapsed while accusing his cardiologist of bugging his pacemaker. For two weeks he lay unconscious in a charity ward at Kings County Hospital, his mouth locked in a silent scream, like the figure in the woodcut by Munch. Then he died.

I had married Maggie and was working in Manhattan. Two days after the memorial service I took the subway over to Brooklyn, to Uncle Danny's shul. Uncle Arthur sat alone before the ark. I sat down beside him. His voice broke as he talked about the brother who was his best friend, his only friend. The words came out thick and smoky and strangely eloquent as they echoed in the vast sanctuary of the nearly empty synagogue. I gripped his hand and held my breath against the tears.

I looked at the curtain hiding the Torah. The Lion of Judah was embroidered on the red velvet in tarnished gold thread. Winter light fell gray and toneless through the windows. The eternal flame flickered fitfully overhead. A scattering of old men mumbled the words of the morning service, swaying to the rhythm of their own prayers. The word *Adonai*, the name of the Lord, emerged now and then from the jumble of Hebrew.

"I'm getting things ready for my birthday next month," he said. The skin stretched tight over his face, his beard thicker and grayer. He looked smaller without Uncle Danny. "Breakfast, go to temple, then start a one-man party. I'll drink a little wine and eat grapes and cake and the candy Harry sent me. I'll look at my birthday cards and my mother's picture on the wall, and sing a Happy Birthday to me. It would be perfect if Danny was there."

After the service, we rode the F train to the Lower East Side. We'll prowl the streets, I had told Uncle Arthur, stalking the past. "Maybe we'll find the sign over your father's old shop," I said. When we reached Orchard Street it seemed possible to come upon Simon around any corner. Uncle Arthur stopped at number ninety-eight, the place where he grew up. The front door to the tenement was boarded up, the windows covered with metal sheets. He pointed to the roof. "That's where Leo used to sit all the time," he said. "He'd throw pennies to us down in the street." I looked up and saw a Chinese man in a white parka. The past was there, but only just visible beneath the scrim of the present.

"See you later," I said at the Second Avenue subway stop.

"What does that mean? My super says that, too."

"I'll see you in a while."

"But later? That could be an hour. Do you mean I'll see you sooner?"

"Maybe."

"What do you call things like that?"

"Expressions. It's just an expression."

"Well, it's a funny expression. What does it mean? Later? Sooner? It doesn't mean anything."

"You're right."

"So when will you see me again?"

"Sooner or later."

I hugged Uncle Arthur, squeezing the dust out of his jackets. He seemed to be made of nothing but dust. I watched him go down into the subway, hoping that he would find a nice pair of shoelaces on the way home.

My father could have used something like a shoelace collection. He'd been married to Shirley for fourteen years. I hardly saw him anymore. It was unpleasant for me to be around him. He lived with Shirley alone now, isolated from Sandy and me and his past. He seemed always mad at something, always on edge, entrapped in a world that kept getting narrower and meaner.

He was now chief of research at an electronics firm in northern New Jersey. Sometimes he took visitors on tours of the plant. He hated that part of the job: It took him away from his research.

He told me that one afternoon he had counted

off the first twenty people in line and told the rest to wait. The guy in front of the second twenty was black. He felt slighted and called my father a racist.

"You're damn right I am," my father snapped. "I'm a mother-fucking honky pig. This is the way I treat all niggers."

He laughed when he told me the story. I didn't. I was appalled, sickened. I couldn't imagine my father saying anything so ugly when I was living with him.

"Come on, Franz," he said. "It's obvious I'm no racist."

"Obvious to who?"

"I took you to civil rights marches in Washington. I read all of Frantz Fanon. I sent the Black Panthers a check for twenty dollars."

"Oh, I see," I said. "You meant it ironically."

"You must have irony-poor blood," he said petulantly.

The old gags didn't work for me anymore. His humor now concealed a bitterness that I didn't know how to remedy and didn't even want to try. Once in a while we'd talk on the phone, but we saw each other less and less. I hadn't seen him for about six months when he called me one evening.

"I've got leukemia," he said, his voice grave.

I didn't know what to say; I didn't say anything.

"Don't worry," he said, "it's not as bad as it sounds."

"It sounds bad."

"Actually, I'm more concerned about my back. I

wrenched it working on the car. No pain, but I can't do my exercises in eleven minutes. I've slowed down to fifteen, so something must have been discombobulated. I'll work back down to eleven soon enough. I'm fitter than I've ever been."

In a week he went into NYU Hospital for the first of several long stays. I went to see him then, but we never had much time alone. Shirley kept a bedside vigil, ministering to him day and night. She gave me twenty minutes at a time, like a prison guard monitoring visiting hours.

I wanted my father to record his reminiscences, and he liked the idea. He would. When I turned on the tape player I thought how much I really was like him. I was putting the distance of his electronic box between him and me. The memories came out in a muddle; my father had never been a model of clarity. There was always one more thought to be sausaged into a sentence. Now his mind was all twists and turns into the cul-de-sacs of an old man nearing death.

The cancer spread quickly, but my father fought it with a force and energy he didn't acknowledge was diminishing. He had no doubt he'd pull through. He had statistical proof. "The studies I've read show I have a seventy-one percent chance of beating this," he said. But this projection was based on error: The doctors hadn't told him he had a chromosomal anomaly that reduced his odds to less than one in three.

The stronger the drugs he had to take, the

weaker he became. Then came the morphine and the hallucinations. He whispered anesthetic incantations. He mistook Sandy for my mother, and me for Uncle Leo. His moods swung wildly and unpredictably—now pensive, now cheerful, now clouded in punsmoke.

He summoned Shirley and me to his bed. We stood on opposite sides.

"The only thing I want . . ." he said, whimpering like a little boy. " . . . is for you and Shirley to be friends. Kiss and make up. I'm begging you." It was not the kind of last wish I thought I'd get from my father. I wanted a blessing, and he was pleading again for reconciliation.

I braced myself for an instant against the rails of the bed. I couldn't give him what he wanted. I fled from the room, forcing myself not to run down the hospital corridor. Life-support machines kept a low, macabre chatter. In every room, in every bed people were swathed in sheets. Small tubes and thin wires connected them to IV poles and electronic devices. Everyone's about to die here, I thought. I stopped at the elevator. "My father's dying," I said aloud. I looked around to see if anyone had heard me. My father's dying, I thought, and I don't want him to. I haven't said everything I want to say to him. I turned back to his room.

Shirley was crouched over my father, holding the tape recorder in front of his face.

"Tell me how much you love me, Sidney," she said.

"Tell me how much I love *me*?"

"No, me. Tell how much you love me."

"I'm me and me is Sidney. I can't be you, can I?"

"Tell me you care for me, Sidney."

"How can I be two persons and yet be the same person?"

"You're Sidney, and you love me, Shirley."

"If I'm not me, who am I? And if I'm somebody else, who can I be?"

"Don't you recognize me?"

"I don't even recognize *me*!"

She persisted, demanding that he affirm his love for her so she'd have it forever. I didn't want to hear any more. I left.

It took Uncle Harry to get me to go back. After Uncle Danny died, he'd come down from Buffalo to live with Uncle Arthur in Brooklyn. "Danny, I could control," Uncle Arthur told me. "But Harry's too much. First of all, he used to be a boxer."

Uncle Harry lacked Uncle Danny's virtues, according to Uncle Arthur. "Harry smokes and he spends a lot of money and he likes hog dogs fried black on both sides!" Uncle Arthur groused. "The easiest way is the best way, he thinks. He never screws the cover back on the juice bottle. It's loose all the time. He gives me candy when he's almost finished with the candy box. He's selfish, selfish, selfish. You got to get him in the mood for this and for that. You can't budge him. He reminds me of that guy tied down by the midgets. What's his name?"

"Gulliver?"

"Yeah, Gulliver."

I'd never met Uncle Harry until the day Uncle Arthur brought him to visit my father in the hospital. My father was asleep when I arrived. Uncle Arthur was poring over a welter of notes written on bank deposit slips. Uncle Harry was reading a medical textbook he obviously found hilarious. Every time he turned a page, he snickered. The book was upside down.

Uncle Harry was decked out in an emerald smoking jacket with his name sewn in black letters on the front and "Retired, Undefeated" on the back. He looked as if he had been prematurely taxidermized, as if his skin had been treated with some preservative, as if he had been taken apart and inelegantly stitched back together.

"My fan club is big in Boston," he said in his mumbly whine. He had a Parliament in his mouth, but no teeth. "In nineteen twenty-two I was president of the Boston Lion's Club. They still call me Champ. In nineteen twenty-eight I won the world ping-pong title in the annex of Gimbels department store in Herald Square. At the nineteen thirty Olympics . . ."

"I didn't know they held Olympics in nineteen thirty," I said.

"Yeah," said Uncle Arthur. "How did that work?"

Uncle Harry dropped somewhat askew into a boxing stance.

"It just worked!"

I wondered about Uncle Harry. Was he really crazy? Or was he just a guy who liked to say whatever popped into his head?

"I was elected Grand Vizier of the Orient," he said.

"When was that?"

"Thousands and thousands of years ago."

He crushed out the Parliament in the palm of his hand. Maybe his asylum didn't have ashtrays.

My father strayed in and out of consciousness. He looked awful. His face was the color of the paper stacked in Uncle Arthur's apartment. He was bald except for a few wisps of hair flying loose and silvery. I covered his head with a Yankees cap. I could hardly bear to touch him. I was still angry and he was dying.

The room had the burnt-umber look of an old photograph. I sat in the failing light and heard Shirley's heels click sharply as she paced the hall, waiting for me to leave. I heard the breath gush from my father's nostrils as he moved in the crisp hospital sheets.

"Benedict," he said. The rasping whisper came out of a twisted mouth and clenched teeth. "I knew you'd keep up the Marrano tradition of practicing Judaism secretly."

I nodded.

"And save your hair clippings and nail parings to take to your grave."

I nodded again.

"You wanted to go to heaven complete, like any self-respecting Jew of your day."

I nodded again.

"Obvious, wasn't it? Or wasn't it? It wasn't in your coffin. All I saw were bones. Bones! But in a bottle with the clippings, with the parings, sealed with wax was living tissue! Live cells! You're my creation, Spinoza!"

My father's head was up, his gown in disarray and his eyes shining.

"I didn't want a Skinner-type, boxed-in replica of my own ideas. I re-created-slash-procreated you as you were, as you are, as you will be. But I couldn't I wouldn't I shouldn't wait thirty years for mental chemical mechanical electromagnetic electronic radioactive simultaneous stimulation amplitude information integrate integrate integrate total observed solid volume chronological limitations explained-slash-contained-slash-normalized-slash-equalized-slash-tenderized English materialist Hobbes and for balance and *for* balance and for *balance* French dualist Descartes . . . Or was it duelist Descartes? . . . Don't you think Man thinks Man drinks Man stinks in atoms in clouds in rocks in in in consciousness exists-slash-persists-slash-resists slash slash slash slash. . . . Don't you think? Don't you? Think! Or don't you?"

My uncles listened to their brother with inexhaustible patience.

"And now and now and *now* I must return to my latest project . . .

"Another Orthodox Jew, a redhead . . .

"He glows with a queer light—and they say he was an excellent carpenter, too."

He set his mouth in a small smile and chuckled softly. His laughter was melodious, and came from all over his face, a small fugue.

I thought of Uncle Arthur dragging in the sacred debris of the city, and Uncle Danny, the prophet of paranoia in the Temple of Junk. I thought of Uncle Harry, the undefeated champion of fantasy, and Uncle Leo spiraling into infinity on his impossible track. My father was the brother of his brothers, I realized. And I was his son, sole heir to this lunatic legacy.

He recognized me.

"Hey, Franz," he said. "Remember the time at Yankee Stadium when Mickey Mantle tried to kill Danny?"

I looked at my uncles. I looked at my father. I took his hand.

How could I forget?

ABOUT THE AUTHOR

Franz Lidz lives 600 yards north of the Mason-Dixon Line with his one wife, (Maggie), two daughters (Gogo and Daisy Daisy) and three llamas (Edgar, Ogar and Vanessa Shakehips).

By the year 2000, 2 out of 3 Americans could be illiterate.

It's true.

Today, 75 million adults...about one American in three, can't read adequately. And by the year 2000, U.S. News & World Report envisions an America with a literacy rate of only 30%.

Before that America comes to be, you can stop it...by joining the fight against illiteracy today.

Call the Coalition for Literacy at toll-free **1-800-228-8813** and volunteer.

Volunteer Against Illiteracy. The only degree you need is a degree of caring.